Sue Dibb is co-director of the Food Commission and regularly writes for newspapers and magazines, including *BBC Vegetarian Good Food Magazine*. She has contributed to numerous books, radio and television programmes. Her book on food labelling, *What the Label Doesn't Tell You*, was published in 1998.

Tim Lobstein is also co-director of the Food Commission and is a founder of the non-profit Food Information Trust. He has written many books on the subject of food, including *Fast Food Facts*, *Teach Yourself Healthy Eating for Babies and Children* and *The Nursery Food Book*. Tim has contributed to many other books and is a regular contributor on radio and television news.

The Food Commission is the leading consumer watchdog on food issues in the UK. Founded in 1988 and funded by public subscription, it is entirely independent of the food industry and the government. The Food Commission campaigns for safer, healthier food in Britain and publishes a quarterly investigative journal, *The Food Magazine*.

GM
FREE

GM
FREE

A shopper's guide to genetically modified food

BY SUE DIBB &
DR TIM LOBSTEIN

WITH HUGH WARWICK
& RACHEL SUTTON

First published in Great Britain in 1999 by
Virgin Publishing Ltd
Thames Wharf Studios
Rainville Road
London W6 9HT

A catalogue record for this book is available
from the British Library.

ISBN 0 7535 0388 3

Designed and typeset
by Roger Kohn Designs

Printed by Mackays of Chatham plc

Contents

Acknowledgements

Thanks to Sandra Bell of Genetic Engineering Alliance for her constructive comments on an early draft of this book, and to Ian Tokelove and Mary Whiting of the Food Commission for providing invaluable office support.

We would also like to thank the food manufacturers, wholesalers and retailers who provided prompt and helpful answers to our questions, especially those who have themselves been conducting surveys of GM-free suppliers and whose experience was of great help to us.

We are also indebted to the work being done by the organisations, campaigns, groups and societies who are keeping the issue of genetic modification at the top of the public agenda, and who gave us information and support for this book.

Finally, we're immensely grateful to David Gould, our editor at Virgin, for his inspiration and support – and for making all the non-genetic modifications necessary to bring this book to fruition.

Preface

Regular headlines about genetically modified (GM) food leave many of us anxious and confused about what we are eating. We're promised food that is better for our health, good for the environment and a solution to the problems of world hunger. But what are the facts? Gene science is already transforming the food on our plates, but will these new foods bring benefits – or is it an experiment in which we are all guinea pigs? It's hard to know who to believe.

But one thing is certain. We need more information, and we need information we can trust. At the Food Commission we've been bringing consumers the facts about the food they eat for over ten years. As an independent consumer organisation we are well respected for the impartiality of our information and advice.

Using straightforward language, this book gives you the information you need to make up your own mind on the GM debate. In Part 1, we separate the myths from the facts, look at the issues behind the headlines, tell you which foods are made with GM ingredients and explain why reading labels is not always enough to tell you what you're eating.

In Part 2 of GM FREE, we print the results of the biggest survey ever conducted on GM ingredients in food. We've contacted all the major companies – retailers, manufacturers and organic producers – and got them to tell us exactly what is in their food. We asked: Do you use GM ingredients? If so, do your labels tell the consumer about them? And are there any products you can **guarantee** to be GM free? The result is a clear and comprehensive list of a large range of everyday foods, enabling you to check out all your favourite brands for GM ingredients.

While we were preparing this book, a growing number of supermarkets and food companies decided to join consumers in saying no to GM ingredients. And because we know that company policies change, in Part 3 of GM FREE we've provided the phone numbers of every single company we contacted, plus others, so you can get in touch directly to find out about any changes. For readers wanting to know more about particular aspects of GM food and the technology behind it, we've provided contact details for a range of organisations, from government departments to gene-food companies, as well as pressure groups. And because we can't go into every aspect of the technology in this book, we also provide a list of further-reading suggestions.

We've gone to great lengths to ensure that this book is as up to date and accurate as possible – all the information in Part 2 has been supplied direct by the manufacturers, wholesalers and retailers responsible for our food – but product formulations may change, and it is possible that by the time this book reaches the shops some of the foods listed here may have changed their ingredients.

Sue Dibb & Dr Tim Lobstein
April 1999

Introduction

Genetic engineering has been described as the most powerful tool yet developed for the manipulation of nature. For better or worse, it is changing the world. Genetic engineering holds out the promise of unprecedented improvements in the variety and quality of our food, solutions to global food problems, improved health and medicines, and the creation of new 'clean and green' industries that are much kinder to the environment. Clearly, if such promises bear fruit, genetic engineering will indeed offer substantial benefits for the human race.

However, many people feel that it is too early to tell whether the biotechnology revolution will live up to all its promises. Most people feel that much more research is needed to resolve the two key questions: Are genetically modified (GM) foods safe to eat? And what effect does genetic modification have on the environment?

Public concerns reached fever pitch early in 1999, with newspaper headlines condemning so-called 'Frankenstein foods' and government ministers dismissing much of the reporting as 'hysterical'. But behind the headlines lie serious issues about the safety of GM food, concerns for the environment and the way in which decisions about GM food are taken. The *Financial Times*, not known for its hysterical reporting, summed up the criticisms as follows: 'The government's handling of the issue has been characterised by cosy commercial relationships, ministerial confusion and a disregard for official environmental advice.' (5 February 1999.)

Whether or not these concerns are justified, it seems clear that some aspects of the technology, such as those used to diagnose and treat disease, will be more easily accepted by the general public than those that seem to offer dubious benefits for consumers. There is clearly a delicate balance to be struck between the biotech companies' need to innovate and the need to regulate this new and potentially harmful technology to protect consumers and the environment.

The rush to cash in on the fruits of genetic modification, spearheaded by powerful multinationals, means that we are already eating some of the products of this relatively untested technology. Only recently have people noticed that GM food has ended up on our plates without our realising it. For the British public, made aware of food-safety issues by outbreaks of E coli food poisoning and the crisis over the cattle disease BSE, the prospect of GM foods being introduced 'on the quiet' touched a raw nerve.

Gene technology may well improve the quality of our lives and the world we live in, but right now we cannot be sure. In the meantime, we should proceed with caution. At the very least, consumers want better labelling of GM foods, better regulation of GM processes and, above all, more information so that they can make up their own minds.

Part 1
MODIFIED FOOD

What is GM Food?

Genetically modified (GM) food is the latest food technology to hit the supermarket shelves. It doesn't look, smell or taste any different from any other kind of food. It may have some advantages over traditional foodstuffs, especially in farming and food production – it is certainly revolutionising the way in which food is grown and processed. Few of us, however, have any idea what it is or whether we are eating it.

Genetic modification, also known as genetic engineering, is a technically advanced development of techniques that have been with us for thousands of years. Ancient civilisations such as those in Egypt and Mesopotamia harnessed micro-organisms to alter the structures of foods, for example fermenting fruits and grains with yeast to make wine and beer. They were probably the first to use the methods we now call biotechnology (from the Greek 'bios' meaning life). Cheese and bread are both familiar products of biotechnology.

WHAT ARE GENES?

The characteristics of every living thing, animals and plants alike, are determined by genes, which are the codes for the building blocks of life. They are essentially instructions in the form of DNA (deoxyribonucleic acid), a complex chemical that carries coded information controlling the millions of characteristics that make up every living organism. Genes are found in every cell of a creature or plant, and are passed down from generation to generation – which is why children inherit the characteristics of their parents.

For humans, genes determine physical characteristics such as how tall we will grow or the colour of our eyes. Genes decide what kind of flowers or perfume a plant may have, or whether an animal is a bird or a fish.

WHAT IS GENETIC MODIFICATION?

In the 1980s and 90s, great advances were made in genetic engineering. Scientists started to discover which genes control which characteristics, and to find ways to manipulate them. These genetic changes, and the characteristics they produce, can then be passed on to the next generation. For humans, in the future this knowledge may mean cures for diseases that are genetically determined, such as cystic fibrosis, Huntingdon's disease and some cancers. For agriculture, it already means crops that contain toxins to kill pests, that can resist being sprayed with chemical weedkillers or that can stay fresh longer after harvesting.

Altering the characteristics of plants and animals is not new. Traditionally plants and animals have been cross-bred, so that genes controlling desirable characteristics will be passed on to the offspring. Horses, cattle, pigs and dogs were domesticated in this way, and cereals such as wheat and barley are the product of millennia of human intervention that have turned wild grasses into valuable foodstuffs. This kind of selective breeding is often a hit-and-miss affair, but it has been responsible for producing many thousands of plant varieties and animal breeds over the centuries, including high-yielding crops and farm animals that grow faster or produce leaner meat.

What genetic modification now offers is a speedier version of traditional breeding techniques to select desired characteristics. For example, in 1993 in Australia, 'superpigs' which grow faster and produce leaner meat were patented.

But genetic engineering is more than just a speedier version of traditional breeding techniques. It opens up possibilities that traditional methods never could. Genes can be added, inactivated or deleted from cells and, in the most revolutionary branch of genetic engineering, they can be transferred from one species to another, to produce new 'transgenic' organisms. In nature you can't cross a fish with a vegetable. Working in the laboratory, researchers have successfully added the gene that protects a type of flounder from the cold into the genetic code of a tomato to produce a tomato that is frost resistant.

HOW THEY MODIFY GENES

Scientists use chemicals called enzymes to remove a selected gene from the DNA of a plant, animal or bacterium. They can then insert this gene into the DNA of simple creatures such as yeasts or bacteria to duplicate them many times. 'Gene transfer systems' are used to introduce these genes into the new cells, most commonly using a bacterium or virus, or alternatively a 'gene gun' can be used to shoot tungsten or gold particles coated with DNA into plant tissue.

The new genes won't work unless something called a 'promoter' is inserted alongside the gene. This 'switches on' the gene so that it produces the desired characteristic. The most commonly used promoter is a gene from a virus, often from the 'cauliflower mosaic virus'. This promoter is used in 90% of GM crops. Although considered to be safe, there are suggestions that this promoter might be responsible for the unexpected changes in rats found in the experiments of Dr Arpad Pusztai (see pages 22–23).

Although genetic engineering is often described as a precise technology, it can in fact be a hit-and-miss affair with no certainty as to where the new gene will end up in the genetic sequence of a plant or animal, or what side effects its insertion may cause. Critics say this makes its effects hard to predict and opens up the possibility of unexpected chemical changes that could affect human health.

Because attempts to transfer genes often have a low success rate, 'marker genes' are added to the genetic material to identify whether a gene transfer has been successful. Most commonly, these have been genes that confer resistance to an antibiotic. Dosing the cells with the antibiotic weeds out the successful transfers by killing off those in which gene transfer was not successful, but the use of these 'antibiotic-resistance marker genes' is raising safety concerns about the spread of antibiotic resistance.

A BRIEF HISTORY OF GM FOOD

In the nineteenth century, Gregor Mendel, a monk from Moravia (now part of the Czech Republic), first described how characteristics are inherited when he studied garden peas. But the word 'genetics' was not coined until 1905. The real breakthrough in modern molecular biology came in 1953, when James Watson and Francis Crick first identified the double-helix structure of DNA. Since then there has been a revolution in scientists' understanding of how genetic information is expressed within cells and passed between generations.

This knowledge has led to commercial applications both in the field of medicine – early products of genetic modification such as human insulin were in use from the early 1980s – and the field of agriculture and food production.

The US is leading the world in the growing of genetically modified crops. Several varieties of GM soya and maize, as well as tomatoes, potatoes, papaya and squash (pumpkin), have all been given the go-ahead. And, whether we realise it or not, we are now eating the products of some of these crops. GM tomatoes, soya and maize (corn) are now imported into Europe. GM tomatoes are being used in

THE COMPANIES BEHIND GM FOODS

There are some 2,800 biotechnology companies worldwide – many of which have grown out of university departments – but a handful of multinational corporations is increasingly dominating the market. These corporations typically comprise an agrochemical division (making chemicals such as pesticides and weedkillers), a seed company, a food-processing company and a veterinary-products or pharmaceutical company. Genetic developments in one part of the company are often used to generate markets and profits for another part of the company. For example, herbicide-resistant GM crops help sell more of the company's herbicide.

tomato purée, while ingredients from GM soya and maize are being used in a huge range of processed food products.

Landmarks
1983 First transgenic plant, a tobacco plant given a marker gene, is created
1990 First genetically modified organism (GMO) to be used in food, a modified yeast, approved in UK
1992 First food to be made from a genetically modified ingredient goes on sale in the UK – a vegetarian cheese
1996 Sainsbury's and Safeway introduce GM tomato paste
● EU approves importation, and first shipments of GM soya from the US arrive in Europe
1997 Iceland Frozen Foods bans GMOs from own-label foods
1998 EU rules on labelling of GM soya and maize agreed
● UK government announces new monitoring of effects of GM crops
1999 A growing number of supermarkets, food companies, fast-food retailers and caterers pledge to remove GM ingredients from their products.

MONSANTO is the US company behind the soya genetically modified to be resistant to the company's herbicide, Roundup, and now in many foods on our supermarket shelves. The company has also developed insect-resistant GM potatoes, maize and cotton, which are all grown in the US.

Monsanto is the world's second biggest seed company and the third largest in agrochemicals. Roundup is the world's biggest-selling weedkiller. Monsanto also has food interests: the artificial sweetener NutraSweet, used in a huge range of diet, low-calorie, reduced-sugar foods and drinks, is probably its best-known brand. Its veterinary-medicines arm markets a milk-boosting hormone for cattle, bovine somatotropin (BST), which is a product of gene technology.

In the UK, Monsanto gained a high media profile after launching an extensive advertising and information campaign in 1998 designed to persuade the public of the benefits of genetic engineering. But following the campaign a leaked consultants' report to the company noted: 'The latest survey shows an on-going collapse of public support for biotechnology and GM foods. At each point in this project, we keep thinking that we have reached a low point and that public thinking will stabilise, but we apparently have not reached that point.'[1] Earlier, Monsanto had apologised to consumers in Europe for underestimating their concerns about the way GM soya was introduced.

NOVARTIS was formed in 1996 by the merger of Swiss companies Sandoz and Ciba-Geigy, making it the world's largest life-science company, its second largest seed firm, third largest pharmaceutical firm and fourth largest veterinary-medicine company. Novartis's best-known products are probably the 'quit smoking' nicotine-replacement therapy Nicotinell and the bedtime drink Ovaltine. It has developed a GM maize that is toxic to the European corn borer pest and also resistant to the company's herbicide, Basta. Ingredients derived from this maize are now in foods on our supermarket shelves. It has also developed other strains of GM maize.

ZENECA, which was previously ICI's life-science division, is a British company behind the GM tomato purée on sale in some supermarkets. The delayed-ripening tomatoes used in this are currently grown in the US, but the company intends to grow the crop in Spain or Italy by the year 2000, if granted regulatory approval. The company says its next big launch will be GM bananas, grown in Central America or the Caribbean to resist a fungal disease. It is not anticipated that any fruit from these plants will be on sale in Europe until 2006. Zeneca has conducted limited field trials of GM maize, oilseed rape and sunflower in the UK and elsewhere in Europe,[2] and is now conducting trials on potatoes.

Zeneca is the world's fourth largest agrochemical company and is involved in pharmaceuticals. Among its pharmaceutical products are the blood-pressure drug Inderal and the antimalarial Paludrine. It also owns Advanta, the world's fifth largest seed corporation.

AGREVO, a German company, has developed oilseed rape that is tolerant of the herbicide glufosinate-ammonium. It is likely to be the first GM crop to be grown commercially in the UK. The company also has a herbicide-resistant GM maize, which is grown in the US and Canada, and oilseed rape grown in Canada.

CALGENE is a Californian company founded in 1980 to develop genetic engineering for agriculture. It was the company behind the delayed-ripening GM Flavr Savr tomatoes grown in the US after it was commissioned by Campbell's Soups to develop a tomato that stayed firmer for longer. Calgene is also experimenting with high-sweetness GM strawberries, and has produced specialist oils from GM canola.

Other companies developing GM crops include Pioneer Hi-Bred, Du Pont and Dow Chemicals.

Genetic modification of food represents only a small proportion of the research undertaken by British biotech companies: far more companies are developing genetically engineered pharmaceuticals and methods for diagnosing diseases. Although there is public support for the medical uses of GM, there are fears that these achievements are being overshadowed by the row over genetically modified food.

WHAT GM FOODS ARE ALREADY ON SALE IN THE UK?
No GM crops are yet grown commercially for food in the UK, although many trials are under way. However, we are already eating several kinds of GM food made from crops grown in the US. Here is what is on the supermarket shelves:

Tomato purée

Tomato purée made from genetically modified tomatoes grown in the US is on sale in Safeway and Sainsbury's under their own label. At the time of writing, Sainsbury's has announced it will not be restocking the product, in line with its GM-free own-brand policy. The tomatoes have been engineered to remain firmer after picking, which, according to the manufacturers, makes the purée cheaper to produce. There are no legal requirements for these products to be labelled, but the supermarkets label the tomato purée voluntarily.

The purée has also been approved in the UK to be used in a wide range of processed food, such as pizzas, but the extent to which it is used is not known.

Soya

GM soya, modified by Monsanto to be resistant to its weedkiller, glyphosate (Roundup), has been imported from the US since 1996. The US producers do not segregate GM soyabeans from conventional soyabeans, so it is difficult for manufacturers to tell whether the soya ingredients they use contain GM beans. Soya and its derivatives, such as oil, flour, protein and lecithin, are used in well over half of all processed foods, from bread and biscuits, chocolate and cakes to meat alternatives and ready meals. Unless manufacturers use guaranteed non-GM soya, a vast number of products will contain small amounts of GM soya. Only some GM soya ingredients need to be labelled.

Maize

The first GM maize (corn) to be approved for use in Europe has been developed by the company Novartis to be resistant to insects and to the weedkiller glufosinate. It contains a gene from a bacterium, *Bacillus thuringiensis* (Bt), which is toxic to a common pest, the European corn borer. Maize is used in many foods and drinks, including breakfast cereals, snack foods, processed foods and pet food. It is also a source of fructose which is used in soft drinks and confectionery, and is used in animal feed as well.

Cheese
Much cheese is made using a GM enzyme called chymosin instead of traditional rennet, which comes from calves' stomachs. Chymosin is used in many vegetarian cheeses and increasingly in hard cheeses for general consumption. At the time of going to press, the Co-op CWS is the only company to label its vegetarian cheese as GM.

Enzymes
GM enzymes are already used to make a large number of products, including drinks, bakery goods and dairy products. None are labelled.

Yeast
A GM yeast for making bread and a brewers' yeast have been approved, but it is difficult to know the extent to which they are used commercially.

Vitamin B2 (Riboflavin)
Riboflavin produced from genetically modified micro-organisms has been approved, but it is not known how widely it is being used. Vitamin B2 is often added to breakfast cereals, soft drinks, baby foods and slimming foods.

WHAT'S ON THE WAY
The majority of GM crops are being modified to be resistant to weedkillers (e.g. Monsanto's GM soya), insects (e.g. Novartis's GM maize), or other plant disease, offering farmers an easier way to get good harvests. Some, such as GM tomatoes, have a longer shelf life after harvesting. Also in the pipeline are pineapples that stay fresher for longer, slow-ripening bananas and other crops with a longer shelf life.

The next GM foods to reach British supermarkets are likely to be from crops already tested in Europe or from GM crops already grown commercially in the US and Canada. These could be whole tomatoes, potatoes, sugar beet and radicchio, but they would first need European approval.

GM oilseed rape (known as canola in the US) is likely to be the first crop allowed to be grown in the UK. Oil from oilseed rape is used as frying oil, and is in margarines and spreads, dressings and mayonnaise. Various GM varieties of oilseed rape, maize and chicory are awaiting European approval.

We are also being promised 'nutraceuticals' – foods that are healthier for us, such as potatoes with more starch (so that chips absorb less fat when cooked) and low-caffeine, high-aroma coffee beans. Fruits may be produced without unwanted pips, while there are plans to modify strawberries to make them sweeter.

But it is not just crops that are being modified. Research is also focusing on animals. Over twenty species of fish, including rainbow trout, salmon and carp, have now been genetically modified in the laboratory to make them grow faster or bigger, although it is likely to be some years before these techniques are perfected.

Research on farm animals, including pigs, cattle, sheep and poultry, is concentrating on ways to make them grow faster, be more resistant to disease or produce better-quality meat. 'Dolly', the world's first genetically modified cloned sheep, became a media star in 1997 but raises the possibility of producing herds of cloned, identical, genetically modified animals in the future. Meanwhile, cows are being encouraged to produce more milk via an injectable growth hormone made using gene technology, known as bovine somatotropin (BST). BST is allowed to be used in the US but is currently banned in Europe.

IT'S NOT JUST FOOD

Food is only part of the biotech revolution. Apart from developments in the medical uses of genetic engineering to identify diseases, pharmaceutical and chemical companies are also investing in technology that blurs the boundaries between medicine and farming. The term 'pharming' is being used to describe these potentially lucrative biotechnological developments.

Genetically engineered plants and animals, dubbed 'bio-reactors', are being developed to produce medicinal products. Transgenic breeds of sheep, goats and cows can secrete human proteins in their milk which can later be extracted and used in the pharmaceutical industry for the treatment of diseases. Sheep are already producing milk containing a protein used to treat the lung disease emphysema, and goats are producing milk with a human antibody useful in cancer therapy. Dairy cows have been engineered to produce a low-lactose, more digestible milk, and other cows have been bred with human genes so that their milk is more like human breast milk. Researchers are also looking into the possibilities of genetically engineered animal organs (known as xenotransplants) designed for human transplantation, and of inserting human DNA into animals to produce human blood plasma.

WIDE-RANGING BENEFITS

Even more revolutionary are likely to be edible vaccines to confer immunity to diseases such cholera, diarrhoea and hepatitis B. Scientists are already experimenting with bananas and potatoes to deliver these vaccines, which could eliminate the world's medical scourges in a cheap, palatable and highly effective form.

The chemical industry is also investigating the use of GM plants as 'biorefineries' to synthesise products such as industrial oils, pharmaceutical proteins, and enzymes for animal feed and industry. In the US, biotech firms have introduced a gene from the Californian bay tree into oilseed rape plants. The resulting transgenic plants produce lauric acid, which is used to make soap.

The Carnegie Institute in Stanford, California, has introduced two genes from a bacterium into plants to produce PHB, one of the raw materials from which biodegradable plastic is made. GM plants and bacteria are also being developed that can help clean up toxic wastes from industry, and we are promised cotton that is genetically modified to be blue to avoid the need for environmentally damaging chemical dyes.

Future developments could bring environmental benefits including reducing our dependence on fossil fuels such as petroleum and natural gas, making greater use of the sun's energy, and creating a wide range of biodegradable materials, leading to the production of less toxic waste.

GOOD FOR BUSINESS; GOOD FOR US?

'The benefits of biotechnology, today and in the future, are nearly limitless,' says Monsanto, one of the world's leading biotechnology companies. 'Experts assert that biotechnology innovations will triple crop yields without requiring any additional farmland, saving valuable rainforests and animal habitats. Other innovations can reduce or eliminate reliance on pesticides and herbicides that may contribute to environmental degradation. While still others will preserve precious groundsoils and water resources.'[3]

Genetic modification clearly offers enormous commercial opportunities. It has been estimated that the world market for products made using genetic modification will be worth £70 billion by the year 2000, and that nearly three-quarters of this predicted growth will come from food and agriculture.[4] Already, in 1999, about half the US soya and a third of the US maize harvest will come from GM plants.[5]

GM foods do offer some advantages for consumers: vegetarians can now more easily choose 'vegetarian' cheese thanks to GM enzymes that can replace rennet from calves' stomachs, while GM tomato purée is sold at a cheaper price than the ordinary version. Perhaps we will also see GM foods that are lower in fat or higher in vitamins, although insiders predict it will be several years before the first such designer foods hit the supermarket shelves.

ENTER THE TERMINATOR

One of the much heralded benefits of GM crops is that they will help to feed the world. Since the world's population is likely to double in the next fifty years, such claims certainly sound attractive. Crops genetically engineered to withstand drought or disease could mean fewer losses and a possible solution to the constant threat of famine that casts a shadow over many parts of the world. But world hunger is not simply caused by insufficient food: many complex political, social and economic factors are involved.

Critics say that the patenting of crops that goes with genetic engineering may actually be a threat to the world's food security, damaging farmers' livelihoods and reducing the range of food crops that are grown in the world. Some genetically modified crops may in future carry a 'terminator' gene that means the crop will grow for one season but will produce only sterile seeds. Instead of saving seed to grow the following year (as is traditional in many developing countries) farmers will have to buy fresh seed from the manufacturers every year. A variant of this is 'verminator technology', which kills a crop unless the plants are sprayed with a proprietary agrochemical.

Another concern is that, if genetic engineering is used to produce substitutes for raw materials such as sugar, coffee, palm oil and cocoa butter, the economies of many of the world's poorer countries could be devastated.

Is GM Food Safe to Eat?

Whatever benefits GM food might bring to the world, the questions that most people want answered are:

● Is the GM food on my plate safe to eat?
● Do GM crops damage wildlife and the environment?
● What about the moral and ethical issues posed by the technology of genetic modification?

ARE GENE FOODS SAFE?

Everyone wants to be sure that the food on their and their children's plates is safe to eat. In the UK, mad-cow disease (BSE) and outbreaks of food poisoning have made us especially wary about the safety of our food.

GM foods go through a safety approval process before being allowed on our plates. The effect of gene modifications can, however, be hard to predict. After all, the BSE crisis showed us that what may look like simple changes in food production can have devastating effects in years to come. That's why consumer and environmental organisations argue for extreme caution in our approach to all these new foods.

WHAT THE GOVERNMENT DOES

All foods sold in the UK are subject to the Food Safety Act 1990, which requires that foods are fit for human consumption and not injurious to health in any way. Many specific rules cover the way in which food can be made and sold. Additives, for example, may be permitted only in certain foods and at certain quantities, and there are safety levels set for possible contaminants in food, like lead or other harmful substances. Furthermore, the way food is described and labelled is subject to strict rules.

GM foods are subject to additional regulations controlling

which foods we should be allowed to eat and which crops can be grown. In the early 1970s, the UK was in fact one of the first countries to regulate biotechnology when scientists called for a voluntary moratorium until a number of safety questions had been addressed. At the time it was only possible to modify micro-organisms in the laboratory. In 1975 a working party of the House of Lords[6] recommended that genetic-manipulation techniques should be allowed to proceed only with rigorous safeguards.

The report concluded that the technology would provide 'substantial (though unpredictable) benefits' and recommended containment to protect the public at large and precautionary measures to protect those working in the laboratories. The general environment, including plants and animals, was not considered at that time. As 'containment' assumed neither escape nor release from a laboratory, new regulations needed to be drafted once plants and animals were being genetically modified. In the UK this led to the establishment in 1990 of the Advisory Committee on Releases to the Environment (ACRE).

The British government is advised on GM food and crop growing by three different committees of experts:

The Advisory Committee on Releases to the Environment (ACRE) assesses the release and marketing of all genetically modified organisms. Its principal role is to advise the Department of Environment, Transport and the Regions about the risks that might arise from the release of GMOs and to consider applications from companies. It has given more than 120 consents for the experimental release of GMOs in the UK, including commercial growing to produce seeds, although it has not yet approved any crops to be grown for food use.

The Advisory Committee on Novel Foods and Processes (ACNFP) advises both the Ministry of Agriculture, Fisheries and Food (MAFF) and the Department of Health, although in future it will be responsible to the new Food Standards Agency. The committee considers all aspects, including safety, of irradiated and novel foods, including genetically modified foods. It is this committee that decides which GM foods can be allowed on to our plates.

The Food Advisory Committee (FAC) reports to MAFF and is responsible for deciding on a wide range of issues concerned with food safety and food quality, and labelling practices, including the labelling of genetically modified food.

Prime Minister Tony Blair is confident that his government follows the best scientific advice when reaching decisions. 'There is no GM food that can be sold in this country without going through a very long regulatory process,' he has said.[7] Despite these reassurances, criticisms of the current system have been raised:

● The scientific evaluation is based on evidence supplied by the companies wishing to have their products approved
● There are questions about the independence of committee members, some of whom may have links with the food industry. For example, it has been claimed that many of ACRE's thirteen members have direct links with the biotechnology industry[8]
● Chemical differences may be very small and not identified in tests, therefore leading to a false assumption of safety. Some scientists believe that GM foods should be more thoroughly tested, using similar standards to those required for new drugs or food additives
● There is no monitoring required of the long-term effects of gene foods in the population, and ACRE does not consider the cumulative, indirect or long-term effects of GM crops on the environment
● The legislation contains little or no reference to any legal liability if any damage is caused to human health or the environment
● Processing aids such as enzymes are excluded from the approval process
● The split in responsibilities between at least four different government departments (Agriculture, Health, Environment

and Trade and Industry) has made it difficult for the government to create a coherent overall strategy.

There is evidence that the government has been listening to some of these criticisms and, at the time of going to press, changes are being planned. Wildlife specialists are to be brought on to ACRE and the committee's remit will be broadened to consider possible side effects that GM crops may have on the environment (see page 26).

THE EUROPEAN PICTURE
Increasingly, decisions are being taken about our food at a European level. The European Union's stance on the control of genetically modified organisms (GMOs) is largely contained in two pieces of legislation (Directives). The Deliberate Release Directive (90/220) was published in 1990, has been amended twice and at the time of writing is in the process of a third major overhaul. This legislation covers marketing authorisation of GM foods. It was primarily intended as a measure to protect the environment, rather than as a human health-and-safety measure.

The Novel Food Regulation (258/97) came into force in 1997. It went through fourteen redrafts and has been described as a 'collection of loopholes'. This measure addressed the labelling of GM foods but did not apply to the many foods (such as GM soya) that had already been approved under the Deliberate Release Directive. Even for those foods that did fall under its umbrella, it required labelling only if products were not 'substantially equivalent' to existing products (see page 21). Subsequently, under intense consumer and political pressure, the EU agreed new labelling requirements (Directive 1139/98) (see page 38).

The EU has already approved eighteen GMOs[9] but has recently turned down a number of approvals for GM crops. In the face of growing public anxieties about GM foods, EU regulators are becoming more cautious.

Some European countries have taken an independent

stance. Austria and Luxembourg, worried about the spread of bacterial antibiotic resistance, have refused to allow the sale of GM maize produced by the company Novartis – even though it has already been given approval at a European level. Greece has banned the import and marketing of GM oilseed rape, and Sweden has banned genetically modified animal feed, but says it may be forced to accept it in the future. France has in effect a moratorium on growing GM crops. In theory, all these bans could be legally challenged by the European Commission, but there is little support for such action.

INTERNATIONAL REGULATION

International trade agreements make it difficult for any country to block the import of GM crops. The US has threatened many countries that, if they restrict the import of GM crops, demand segregation of crops or even require labelling of GM foods, this would constitute a barrier to free trade and could be challenged under internationally agreed World Trade Organisation (WTO) rules. Any further European restrictions on GM crops could provoke a backlash from the US government and North American companies, who are frustrated by what they see as delays and disruptions to their export markets.

There is a recognition of the need for greater international agreement about the trading of GM crops. The UK government advisory committee ACRE, for example, has expressed concerns about the different ways in which GM crops are regulated in different countries and has called for a workable agreement to be developed and agreed at the earliest opportunity.[10] But attempts to do this (most recently at the UN Biosafety Protocol meeting in Columbia early in 1999) fell apart when the participating countries failed to reach an agreement. 'The inability of the 132 countries present at Cartagena to reach agreement reflected a clash between the trade interests of the US and other GM crop exporters, and the environmental concerns of other countries,' reported the *Financial Times*.[11]

THE APPROVAL PROCESS

All new GM foods must first get approval by the government. What this means in practice is that the Advisory Committee on Novel Foods and Processes considers each separate application from a company to introduce a new GM food.

This approval system is based on the principle of 'substantial equivalence'. Put simply, this means that, if the GM food is chemically the same as the traditionally produced variety, then the committee does not require any special safety tests to be carried out. This concept, developed in the US, is widely accepted internationally.

Critics of the system have questioned the scientific validity of substantial equivalence and the tests that companies carry out. These, say critics (including Professor Philip James, a key government adviser on food safety and nutrition), should be more stringent, because the process of genetic engineering can have effects that are hard to predict. This was clearly shown to be the case in the research conducted by Dr Arpad Pusztai, the scientist at the centre of the row over the safety of genetically modified potatoes (see pages 22–23).

PROBLEMS ASSOCIATED WITH GM FOODS

New toxins

The possibility of new toxins occurring in GM foods has been known for some time. In one early experiment, scientists developed a GM potato that was more resistant to crop damage. However, they also found that the levels of the potato's natural toxin, solanin, increased to such a level that the potatoes were poisonous to eat. The problem was identified at the research stage and so posed no threat to human health. Genetic engineering opens the possibility of producing foods with lower levels of natural toxins as well.

Allergies

The unpredictable nature of gene transfer means that GM foods may be more likely to cause allergic reactions. One to two per cent of the population have allergic reactions to certain food types, most commonly to foods such as milk, eggs, peanuts and other nuts, shellfish, fish, soya and cereals such as wheat.

In early experiments in the US, soyabeans genetically modified to be more nutritious used a gene from a Brazil nut.

THE DOCTOR, THE RAT AND THE GM POTATOES

By his own description, Dr Arpad Pusztai is 'a very enthusiastic supporter' of gene technology. He is also acknowledged to be one of the world's leading experts on the subject of lectins, naturally occurring proteins that protect some plants (including the snowdrop) from attack by insect pests. Gene scientists have been experimenting with adding lectins to crops such as wheat, rice, oilseed rape, tomatoes, sunflowers, cabbages and potatoes.

Dr Pusztai, who worked at the Rowett Research Institute in Aberdeen, was looking for a way in which to test GM foods in general for safety, rather than looking specifically at the safety of the GM potatoes used in the experiments. He fully expected his experiments to give the technology 'a clean bill of health'.

So no one was more surprised than him, he has said, when his research appeared to show that rats fed GM potatoes suffered damage to their immune system, had smaller brains and showed damage to vital organs. These findings landed him in the middle of one of the hottest scientific controversies for years, halting his career and damaging his international reputation.

Dr Pusztai fed groups of rats on two strains of potatoes genetically engineered to include a lectin from snowdrop bulbs. A third group was fed potatoes with the snowdrop lectin simply added, while a fourth group ate ordinary potatoes. He has been accused of simply adding a poison (the lectin) to potatoes, but Pusztai had spent many years showing that lectin was safe, except to insects, even at high concentrations. And as proof of this the rats that were

But the process also unintentionally transferred an allergen from the nut to the soyabean, causing the soya to invoke a similar allergic reaction in susceptible people to that caused by Brazil nuts. The product was voluntarily withdrawn from the market, but other problems may not be so easy to identify.

In the UK, a study at Leicester University for MAFF found

simply fed the lectin along with the potato did not show signs of harm. It was the rats fed the GM potatoes that had damaged immune systems and stunted growth.

Pusztai says more research is needed to find out what may be causing this damage, but it appears to be something about the genetic-modification process itself, rather than the specific genetic changes made to the potato.

There have been suggestions that the gene promoter – in this case the cauliflower mosaic virus – used to 'switch on' the lectin gene could be to blame. The virus itself is non-toxic, but some scientists are asking whether this virus could recombine with other viruses and possibly affect humans. Professor Gordon McVie of the Cancer Research Campaign is another scientist calling for more stringent testing of GM foods. 'When modifying food by virus you need to take extra precautions and do extra safety tests because we know that viruses are responsible for about one-fifth of cancers,' he has said.[12]

Dr Pusztai's work doesn't prove that GM foods are unsafe, but it has shown that much more stringent testing of GM foods than previously thought may be required. The case also highlights how little independent research such as Dr Pusztai's there has been into the safety of GM foods.

Despite initial criticism that he had muddled his results, which resulted in his sacking, there was later acknowledgement that Dr Pusztai's results merit further serious consideration. The Royal Society, Britain's leading scientific body, announced in March 1999 that it was asking a team of the country's most eminent scientists to assess the potential toxicity of using genetically modified plants in foods, including Dr Pusztai's research.

that pollen from GM crops collected by bees may lead to allergic problems for those eating honey.[13] It may be a small risk, say the researchers, but the experiment shows how genetic modification of one type of organism can affect an unrelated foodstuff.

On the positive side, many of the genes responsible for producing allergy-causing proteins have been identified and genetic engineering holds out the promise of altering foods to make them less of a risk for allergy sufferers.

Antibiotic resistance

Another health concern that has been raised is the use of antibiotic-resistance genes in GM crops. These are commonly added as 'marker genes' to GM crops to select successfully modified plants from other specimens that have not been changed (see page 5). They are used, for example, in the GM tomatoes used to make GM tomato purée and in Novartis's GM maize. Some observers fear that antibiotic resistance could be passed on to bacteria in the guts of humans and animals eating the GM foods, which could worsen the problem of resistance to life-saving antibiotics.

In 1996 the ACNFP advised the UK government to vote against the approval of Novartis's GM maize on the grounds that its gene for antibiotic resistance posed an unacceptable risk to animals and humans, partly through the use of unprocessed maize in animal feed. The EU eventually overruled the government and gave the go-ahead. The UK government then said it had no powers to stop the import of the maize, although countries such as Austria and Luxembourg have continued to ban its import.

Alternatives are being developed, including using enzymes to remove marker genes once they have done their job in the laboratory. The House of Lords has called for antibiotic marker genes to be phased out 'as swiftly as possible'.[14]

ASSESSING THE RISKS

There is no evidence that any of the genetically modified foods on sale at the moment pose any risk to the health of people eating them. But that is not the same as saying they can be guaranteed to be 100% safe. It is clear that we don't yet have enough evidence.

The government's Chief Scientific Adviser, Sir Robert May, says, 'More research needs to be done. We don't have all the answers. But in the meantime we shouldn't reject GM crops and food out of hand.'[15] Sceptics may not find this reassuring. Many will remember how Sir Robert's former counterpart, Sir Donald Acheson, the Chief Medical Officer at the Department of Health, reassured the public over BSE in 1990. He said then that there was 'no risk' associated with eating British beef. In 1998 he admitted, 'I should not have done that, because the advice of my [expert] groups was that there was a remote risk, not no risk.'[16]

Of course, no food, whether natural or genetically modified, can ever be said to be absolutely safe. We live in a world full of risks, and it can be difficult to keep them in perspective. We are sometimes told that we are far more likely to be run over by a bus than be affected by the chemicals sprayed on our food, contract human BSE from eating beef or suffer ill-effects from eating GM foods – but this is not a useful analogy. If we are careful, we can see the bus coming and avoid it. With GM food it has become increasingly difficult to know whether we are eating it or not.

What is understandable is that people want to be able to make choices for themselves. And while some may feel that any risk to their personal health is so remote as to be not worth worrying about, the majority say they would like the choice to know what the risks are, what they are eating and to avoid GM products if they wish. In a recent survey,[17] 96% of those questioned said they want all products containing genetically modified food to be clearly labelled. 68% were worried about eating GM food, and more than three-quarters believe that there should be a ban on producing GM products until more research is done.

GM Crops and the Environment

Modern farming has transformed the countryside. Greater farming productivity and efficiency has resulted in bigger fields, fewer hedgerows, more chemical sprays and fewer wild flowers, birds and animals.

In farming, too many weeds can mean the harvest will be reduced, as weeds compete with the crop for water, nutrients and light. Crops, as well as the weeds, can be damaged by weedkillers that are sprayed on to fields. Now crops are being genetically engineered to withstand sprays that kill weeds. These GM crops are called herbicide resistant.

GM crops are being promoted as good for the environment, since they need less use of chemicals. Monsanto, for example, says that herbicide-tolerant crops, such as its GM soya, result in a reduction of up to 30% in chemical sprays. And crops that are modified so they contain their own pesticide could mean less chemical pesticides will be needed.

Herbicide resistance is the most profitable area of crop modification, because the GM crops generate demand for herbicides. Often the company that is developing the herbicide-resistant crop is part of the same company that makes the herbicide, as is the case with Monsanto's Roundup Ready soya. Plant Genetics Systems, part of the German company AgrEvo, has produced a number of crops with resistance to its glufosinate herbicides, including a variety of oilseed rape that is likely to be the first GM crop to be grown commercially in the UK for use in food.

INSECTICIDAL CROPS

Many crops are being modified so they produce toxins that kill or repel pests without the need to spray chemical pesticides. Farmers will be able to spray crops with fewer chemicals, saving them money and causing less pollution from chemical sprays and spray drift on to adjoining fields or gardens. There would be fewer cases of accidental poisoning of farm workers using chemical sprays, and consumers would benefit from crops with lower residues of chemicals.

The most commonly used gene is known as the Bt gene. Bt is short for *Bacillus thuringiensis*, a soil bacteria which produces a natural toxin that kills insects. It has been used for many years by organic farmers as a safe, biological means of controlling pests. Now genetic scientists have recognised its potential for creating GM crops that contain their own pesticide.

The Bt gene has been added, for example, to GM maize to make it resistant to a particular pest called the European corn borer. In the US the European corn borer can infest about 24 million hectares and can cause a 20% loss in the harvest. Large quantities of insecticides, with an estimated value of $20–30 million, are used against this pest each year. In the US farmers and gardeners can grow potatoes, produced by Monsanto with the trade name NewLeaf, that are resistant to the Colorado potato beetle. Monsanto has also designed a Bt cotton to control pests called bollworms. Cotton is one of the most heavily sprayed crops in agriculture and is typically sprayed many times in a season.

Experiments are also under way with other insect toxins, including lectins, which are commonly found in plants of the peas-and-bean family. Lectins from snowdrops were the toxins genetically modified into the potatoes that were used in the experiments of Dr Pusztai into GM-food safety (see pages 22–23).

WILL THE INSECTS FIGHT BACK?

While GM crops may bring benefits, there are also concerns that they may have a downside, too. A major concern is the possibility that insects will become resistant to the toxins in the GM crops. It is a part of the natural evolutionary process that pests adapt and many have already evolved to develop a resistance to ordinary chemical sprays; for example, in some parts of the world mosquitoes became resistant to the chemical DDT, making them even harder to control by chemical means. And in the UK a number of plant diseases, including potato blight, are becoming more difficult to control.

This adaptation could occur faster in GM crops than in conventional crops, because the plants produce the toxin continuously. In the US, the Environment Protection Agency has insisted that growers of Bt crops also plant areas of non-GM crops as 'refugia' where pests can survive, in order to dilute the effects of insect resistance. But there is a debate about how large these areas need to be.

Another concern is that GM plants may harm beneficial insects as well as pests. The Soil Association reports that:

● The death rate of lacewing insects (a source of food for birds) was doubled when they were fed on plant-eating larvae raised on genetically engineered maize
● Rapeseed engineered to produce natural insecticide has also been shown to kill not only the target pests – caterpillars and beetles – but also bees
● Ladybirds eating aphids fed on genetically engineered potatoes were found to suffer from shortened life spans and reduced fertility.[18]

ENVIRONMENTAL CONCERNS

The possible impact on the environment of growing GM crops is difficult to estimate. Understanding whether GM crops pose any significant risk means growing the crop experimentally, though this may not replicate the conditions of larger-scale crop production. Environmental organisations argue for extreme caution, as even these crop experiments may cause irreversible environmental changes.

What happens if modified genetic traits, like resistance to weedkillers, are passed to weeds? And will GM crops lead to the even greater loss of wildlife? The British government's scientific advisers on the Advisory Committee on Releases to the Environment (ACRE), who decide what GM crops can be grown, have acknowledged that: 'There is concern about the decline in the diversity and abundance of wildlife within and surrounding farmland ... The introduction of GM crops into commercial agriculture must not contribute further to these declines.'[19]

With GM crops that are resistant to a particular weedkiller, there are fears that spraying the chemical could mean all wild plants being removed from fields. In turn this could lead to a decline in the number of insects and birds that feed on the weeds. This threat to wildlife led the government's official wildlife advisers, English Nature, and the Royal Society for the Protection of Birds to call for a moratorium on the commercial growing of GM crops.

There are also worries that GM herbicide-resistant crops could make the problem of weeds worse. If GM crops cross-pollinate with wild plants that are closely related to them, so-called 'superweeds' that are also resistant to herbicides could be created. Researchers in Denmark have found that herbicide resistance from a GM oilseed rape could spread to weeds[20] and this effect has also been shown to occur with GM sugar beet. In early 1999, ACRE raised concerns that 'unless managed carefully at the farm, transfer of genes via cross-pollination in crops such as oilseed rape will result in herbicide-tolerant and multiple-herbicide-tolerant hybrids. These may be difficult to control ...'[21]

Concerns such as these have led many consumer, wildlife and environmental organisations to call for a moratorium on the growing of GM crops while further research is carried out. The Environment Minister, Michael Meacher, has rejected calls for a moratorium, but at the time of writing the government says it has reached a voluntary agreement with the biotech industry not to start growing GM crops commercially until 2002. This would allow trials to continue.

This freeze should allow more time for observing the results of monitoring GM crops for their environmental impact, a scheme which the government announced in late 1998. Furthermore, an industry group, the Supply Chain Initiative on Modified Agricultural Crops (SCIMAC), is looking at ways of preventing herbicide-tolerant 'superweeds'.

GM AND ORGANIC FARMING

Organic farmers must adhere to very strict controls on the way they farm. For example, they can't use artificial fertilisers or chemical sprays on their fields. Furthermore, organic food is not permitted to contain GM ingredients. One of the concerns of organic farmers and growers is the potential for GM pollen to transfer to organic crops. In 1998, an organic farmer, Guy Watson, went to court to stop trials of GM maize (sweetcorn) from being grown in fields bordering his organic farm in Devon. He lost the case, and fears he may lose his organic status if indeed the GM pollen does contaminate his crops.

In refusing to order the destruction of the GM crop, Environment Minister Michael Meacher said the GM crop 'would not interfere with the sweetcorn crop being grown on the nearby farm'.[22] At the heart of the row is a debate about how far pollen can travel. ACRE, the body that advises the Department of Environment, ruled that a gap of 200 metres between such crops is an acceptable barrier to prevent pollen transfer. This, they say, would result in a maximum of 1 in 40,000 kernels being cross-pollinated. But a more recent report from the National Pollen Research Unit for the Soil Association[23] concludes that cross-pollination by a moderate wind across 200 metres would be in the order of 1 kernel in 93. Furthermore, the researchers concluded that pollen transfer by bees can occur over a distance of several miles.

While GM crops are not yet allowed to be grown for food, the government has given permission for trials of GM crops at over 500 sites around the country. Soil Association Director Patrick Holden says, 'The only way that the government can fulfil its promise to protect organic farmers (and indeed conventional farmers) who wish to provide a GM-free choice for consumers is through a ban on the growing of genetically engineered maize.'[24]

Organic farmers also fear that the use of the Bt gene to make crops resistant to insects could threaten the future of organic farming. As we have seen (see page 27), Bt produces a natural toxin that kills insects and has been used for many years by organic farmers as a safe and natural means of controlling pests. If the Bt gene becomes widespread, insects could adapt and develop a resistance to the toxin, which would no longer be able to kill them. In that case, the safe and environmentally friendly use of Bt could cease to be an option for organic farmers.

ETHICAL PROBLEMS

To add to the arguments about the safety of GM foods, the question of ethics occupies many people's minds.

Prince Charles summed up these concerns when he said, 'At the moment, as is so often the case with technology, we seem to spend most of our time establishing what is technically possible, and then a little time trying to establish whether or not it is likely to be safe, without ever stopping to ask whether it is something we should be doing in the first place.'[25]

Some people consider that genetic manipulation raises the question of whether it is right for scientists to 'play God' with living organisms. Of course, plant and animal breeders over many thousands of years have produced varieties of crops and farm animals that would never have grown or grazed in the Garden of Eden. But, nonetheless, genetic engineering does raise new questions.

Many consumers are concerned that genetic modification is not 'natural'. They might be particularly concerned if genes were to come from animals that they consider sacred or do not eat. The beliefs of some religious groups, such as Jewish, Muslim, Hindu and Buddhist, may be incompatible with gene technology in general, and they may wish to avoid genes from certain animals in particular. And it is understandable that vegetarians might be concerned about eating plant foods containing animal genes, and that just about everyone would find it hard to eat food containing human genes.

In 1992, the Ministry of Agriculture, Fisheries and Food appointed a committee chaired by Reverend John Polkinghorne to consider the moral and ethical questions of gene food. The

Polkinghorne Committee was convened after the ACNFP was asked to rule whether sheep into which human genes were incorporated to produce medically valuable human proteins in their milk could be used for food. It concluded that it was only acceptable to eat animals from failed experiments that had not been genetically modified.

The Committee went on to consider that 'modifications raising particular ethical concerns will be uncommon'[26] and concluded that there was no overriding ethical objection that would prevent the use of human genes in food production. But research for the Consumers' Association[27] shows that consumers do have anxieties that go beyond these narrow considerations. For example, some consumers have moral objections to the patenting of life forms, and others fear that biotechnology companies will come to dominate the world's food supplies – a view supported by the Canadian-based group Rural Advancement Foundation International (RAFI), which is concerned that the world's genetic resources will become concentrated in the hands of just a few large companies. Already a third of the world's seed market is controlled by ten leading companies.[28] And a great number of people are concerned to ensure that genetic modification of animals is not harmful and does not cause any suffering.

ANIMAL WELFARE

Public opinion is more strongly opposed to genetic modification of animals than of plants.[29] Animal-welfare organisations have long campaigned to improve conditions for animals in factory farming, successfully campaigning, for example, to outlaw veal crates, sow stalls and tethers for pigs. Organisations such as the pressure group Compassion in World Farming fear that the production of genetically engineered animals could result in animal suffering. The Royal Society for the Protection of Animals (RSPCA) has called for a halt to genetic engineering when it is detrimental to the health or wellbeing of animals.

Risks to animal welfare from genetic engineering are

difficult to determine and need to be weighed against the benefits. Many would consider that the benefits of increasing meat or milk production does not justify the means. For example, use of the milk-boosting hormone (BST) – a product of gene technology – can lead to mastitis (infection of the cow's udder), lameness, inflammation from the injections, and other health problems.[30]

Other problems have occurred with animal experiments. In Australia, pigs genetically altered to produce extra growth hormone suffered arthritis, gastric ulcers and diabetes.[31] And in the most extreme reported problem to date, the 'Beltsville pigs' at a US government research station in Beltsville – with genes for human growth hormone – developed severe arthritis, had spinal deformities, became blind or cross-eyed and were impotent.[32]

PATENTING

Patents prevent other companies from copying a new product. Companies involved in genetic engineering see patenting of their transgenic organisms as vital to ensure that they will reap the financial benefits of their research and investment. Since 1998 the patenting of life forms has been legal in the European Union. But many people object morally to the patenting of life forms, particularly of genetically modified animals and human genetic material.

Of particular concern is that trade agreements and patenting legislation could restrict the traditional uses of plants in the Third World. For example, the neem tree has been used for centuries in India as a source of insecticide providing an environmentally friendly form of crop protection. Now the chemical companies in the US have taken out patents on recipes for making the solutions. Critics have accused the companies of 'intellectual piracy'.[33]

Meanwhile, 'gene hunters' working for multinational companies continue to prospect for genetic resources in areas of rich biodiversity such as tropical rainforests. The United Nations Convention of Biological Diversity states that companies should share their profits with the countries where they were found. However, it applies only to plants taken from the wild after 1993 and is likely to be hard to police. The Rural Advancement Foundation International (RAFI) believes that the World Trade Agreement on patents and 'intellectual property rights' is against the interests of poorer farmers, and poorer countries, who could lose the benefits of their natural biodiversity.

Labelling and the Law

Shoppers expect to know what they are buying. Food laws protect us from adulterated food and misleading descriptions, and in some cases impose quality standards, such as how much meat should be in a pork sausage or how much orange juice in squash. But we rely considerably on food labelling to help us make choices.

When it comes to genetically modified food, there is almost unanimous agreement, among the public at least, that foods should be labelled. In a poll for the Consumers' Association published in March 1999,[34] 94% of people felt there should be clear labelling on food packaging.

Even when food ingredients that have come from genetically modified plants cannot be detected in the final product, because they have been processed, 92% still felt that these processed ingredients should be labelled. The government also says it supports labelling, and retailers and manufacturers agree that consumers should have the choice. Some retailers have already gone further than the law requires, giving extra labelling to help shoppers.

European law on the labelling of GM foods, known as the Novel Food Regulations, was introduced in May 1997. This says that GM foods or ingredients do not have to be labelled if they are more of less identical (or 'substantially equivalent') to ordinary foods and ingredients. In practice this means that manufacturers and supermarkets need to label only where GM foods or ingredients:

● Are nutritionally or compositionally different (e.g. a potato that has been modified to change its starch characteristics)
● Contain material that might affect health, such as by triggering allergies
● Raise ethical issues (e.g. animal genes in plant foods for vegetarians).
This meant that, before September 1998, none of the foods so

far approved for sale in the UK needed to be labelled, because they have all been deemed to be 'equivalent' to conventional food. And these labelling laws excluded food additives and processing aids such as enzymes, many of which can be made using genetic modification.

But when GM soya started to be mixed with conventional soya and used in thousands of everyday foods without any requirement to label them, there was an outcry across Europe. Shoppers were angry that they were being denied the option to choose between GM and non-GM ingredients, while retailers and food companies were concerned that non-segregation of crops meant they had no choice about what they could put in their foods. Monsanto, the company behind the GM soya, said it had not foreseen this opposition – perhaps because in the US, where labelling of GM foods is not required, consumers have been unaware that GM soya is being used.

Public pressure led in 1998 to new labelling rules being agreed for the whole of the European Union (Regulation 1139/98). From September 1998, foods and ingredients derived from GM soya and maize, and which contain detectable levels of GM material, must now be labelled as 'produced from genetically modified soya/maize'. In addition, companies may declare, if true, that products are GM free.

LOOPHOLES IN THE LEGISLATION
Although a welcome improvement, even these new rules don't mean that everything is labelled. There are three small but important gaps in the legislation:

1 The labelling requirements apply only to soya from Monsanto's Roundup Ready soyabeans and from one particular kind of GM maize developed by the company Novartis. They don't apply to the GM tomato purée on sale in Sainsbury's and Safeway, but both companies label their purée as coming from genetically modified tomatoes on a voluntary basis. It is unclear whether the rules will be extended to other GM foods already on sale, such as tomato purée, or to those that might be in the pipeline

2 The rules apply only when detectable levels of GM material are found in the final product. While GM soya protein or flour, for example, needs to be labelled, most oils, starches and sugars derived from GM crops need not be labelled. That's because there is no genetic material left in the end product after processing

3 The law does not apply to additives such as the commonly used emulsifier additive, lecithin, or to other processing aids such as enzymes, which may be produced by genetic modification.

Some supermarkets are trying to give their customers information about other GM ingredients, such as GM oil, by labelling their products voluntarily. However, this could end up being more confusing for customers, with some companies choosing to label these extra ingredients while others won't.

LABELLING IMPROVEMENTS

To ensure better labelling for GM foods, consumer organisations such as the Food Commission and the Consumers' Association are calling for:

● Labelling that is accurate, meaningful and consistent
● The government to push for better labelling laws, at European and international level, based on full traceability of GM crops, throughout the food chain
● The separation of GM and non-GM crops throughout the supply chain so that food labels can accurately reflect whether they contain ingredients from GM or non-GM crops
● The food industry to use ingredients from non-GM sources so that shoppers can have alternatives to foods containing GM ingredients
● Organic production to be protected from cross-contamination by GM crops, so shoppers can be confident that organic food does not harbour any GM-derived material.

CHECKING THE LABEL

This book lists hundreds of GM-free foods, but choosing GM free will typically mean you need a close look at the label. Even then, the information you will get may be incomplete or inconsistent. Bear the following points in mind when out shopping.

WHAT DOES AND DOESN'T HAVE TO BE LABELLED

GM ingredients that must be declared

- soyabeans
- soya pieces
- soya flour
- tofu
- vegetable or soya extract
- soya protein
- soya protein isolate
- soya concentrate
- textured vegetable protein
- hydrolysed vegetable protein
- maize
- maize flour
- cornflour.

GM ingredients that don't have to be declared

Additives are excluded from the labelling laws and include:
- soya lecithin/lecithin E322, an emulsifier added to a wide range of foods, including chocolate, margarine, breakfast cereals, bread, cakes and biscuits (for full list of additives see page 52).

Other soya or maize ingredients are excluded because the processing removes any of the genetic material. These derivatives include:

Inconsistent labelling policies

Some supermarkets (Sainsbury's and Safeway) have chosen to declare in large print whether their own-brand tomato purée is made from GM tomatoes, but not all producers are so open. You'll need to look at the small print of the ingredients list to discover whether any of the ingredients say they are 'produced

- soya oil, vegetable oil, hydrogenated vegetable oil, vegetable fat
- modified corn starch, used in many processed foods
- glucose syrup, used in confectionery and soft drinks
- dextrose, fructose and maltodextrin, which are types of sugar.

Where you might find GM ingredients

Soya ingredients, in the form of flour, meal, protein, oil and lecithin, are used in up to 60% of processed foods. You'll usually find soya ingredients in:

- bread, biscuits and bakery products
- soya-based drinks
- milk drinks and desserts
- confectionery
- baby and dietetic foods
- meat and vegetarian savoury products
- pet food.

GM maize finds its way into processed food such as flour, flakes, meal, oil, starch, glucose syrup, fructose syrup and dextrins. It is used in:

- baked beans
- tinned pasta
- soups
- sauces
- cakes and biscuits
- packet desserts
- baby foods.

from genetically modified soya/maize'. But as we have seen, some ingredients from GM sources, such as oil or lecithin, don't have to be declared. As a result, even if no ingredients are labelled as being GM, you can't necessarily assume that the product is GM free.

The fact that some companies are choosing to label these ingredients is welcome, but adds to the confusion. If you're not sure about a product, check it against the lists in this book.

Modified starch

This ingredient, a thickener used in many processed foods from baby foods and sauces to pie fillings, has caused extra confusion. Does 'modified starch' mean 'genetically modified starch'? Strictly speaking, it doesn't: the starch has been 'modified' by heat or chemical treatment to improve its uses to food manufacturers – but there's a twist. If the modified starch comes from GM maize then it would be a GM ingredient – except that it is exempt from labelling, so you won't be able to tell.

'GM-free' labels

An increasing number of manufacturers and retailers are committed to producing and selling foods that are not made with GM ingredients. The lists in Part 2 of this book will help you identify GM-free foods and their manufacturers. Organic producers and growers have banned the use of GM crops and ingredients derived from them, so organic foods shouldn't contain, or be made from, any genetically modified material.

Some supermarket chains (see pages 53–60) say that they will avoid using any GM ingredients in their own-brand foods, and other supermarkets are trying to phase them out. The Vegetarian Society has also banned companies wishing to use its 'V' logo from using GM ingredients (with the exception of the cheese rennet substitute, chymosin) in their foods. And an increasing number of manufacturers, particularly those in the health food trade, are working to ensure that their products do not include GM ingredients. You may find such products labelled as 'not made using genetically modified ingredients' or similar words.

Failing the test

Even GM free labels can be unintentionally misleading. In one case, imported organic Tortilla chips did contain detectable levels of GM material.[35] Similarly, Linda McCartney brand vegetarian sausages and mince, which had previously claimed to be from a non-GM source, were found in tests for BBC 2's *Newsnight* programme by public analysts at Worcestershire Scientific Services to contain traces of GM material.[36] It is thought that these cases were due to cross-contamination by GM crops during the growing, transportation or manufacture of non-GM soya, and highlight the unintended risks to organic and conventional production from genetic modification.

The technology for testing whether foods contain genetically modified material has lagged behind the arrival of GM foods on supermarket shelves and new labelling laws, and technology that can reliably detect the presence of as little as 1% GM material in a raw ingredient such as soya or maize flour is relatively new. The tests work by identifying traces either of genes added to the crop or of the proteins they produce. But more accurate analysis is harder when ingredients are used in processed foods such as cake or chocolate.

In February 1999, Worcestershire Trading Standards Services said that, of 200 foods sampled by UK local authorities, about one-third contained traces of GM soya – at the time only one of the products was properly labelled.[37] New requirements being introduced on GM labelling should mean that more foods are correctly labelled.

Food companies have faced great challenges over the introduction of GM labelling, and much confusion still exists over exactly what they should be labelling. While the EU law on labelling GM soya and maize came into effect in September 1998, the details of its enforcement were still being worked out well into 1999. For example, the EU says it will draw up a list of ingredients from GM sources that don't have to be labelled and set a threshold limit below which other ingredients don't have to be labelled. At the time of writing, these have yet to be finalised.

WHAT ABOUT EATING OUT?

When you eat out in a restaurant or café, or buy food from a takeaway, the law says that you should be able to tell whether the food contains GM ingredients – at least the ones that must be labelled in the shops. By September 1999, caterers must indicate to diners, either on the menu or on notices, if there are GM ingredients in dishes; if detailed information is not printed, then staff should be able to give customers more specific information. That's the theory, but it may be some time before all catering establishments are fully complying.

CHOOSING ORGANIC FOOD

It is now much easier to find organic food. Supermarkets are recognising that a growing number of shoppers are looking for organic food and are prepared to pay the higher prices. Many feel that it is a price worth paying to be sure that the food they eat is produced without GM ingredients or harmful chemicals and in a way that is kinder to the environment than conventional farming. And, as more people buy organic food, prices are likely to come down.

By choosing organic food you can be sure that you are choosing food that is not made from GM crops or ingredients. Organic producers are not allowed to grow GM crops, use it to feed their farm animals or add GM ingredients or their derivatives to processed organic foods. Buying organic also means you are avoiding possible pesticide residues and supporting farming that has taken greater care to protect the environment. Organic agriculture relies on crop rotation and natural fertilisers to maintain healthy soil and plants, rather than on chemicals.

And it's not just fruit, vegetables and cereals that are grown organically. Much meat is now produced to organic standards, as well as eggs, milk and other dairy products. The diet of organically reared animals must be natural and wholesome, and the routine use of antibiotics and other drugs is banned.

But what assurances do shoppers have that food that is

labelled as organic really does live up to these standards? While you may see food on supermarket shelves described as 'traditional', 'natural' or 'environmentally friendly', the only description that is guaranteed by law is 'organic'. In addition, all producers and processors of organic food must be registered and regularly inspected.

The government agency responsible for approving the organic bodies which register organic farms and processors is the United Kingdom Register of Organic Food Standards (UKROFS). There are six organic bodies approved by UKROFS:

● The Soil Association
● Organic Farmers and Growers
● Organic Food Federation
● Biodynamic Agricultural Association
● Scottish Organic Producers Association
● Irish Organic Farmers and Growers Association.

You may see their logos on organic produce, sometimes alongside a supermarket's own organic labelling.

WHERE TO FIND ORGANIC FOOD

● Supermarkets are stocking an increasing range of organic foods. Sainsbury's and Waitrose have the largest selection
● Organic supermarkets. There are two organic supermarket chains: Out of this World (in Nottingham and Newcastle) and Planet Organic (in London, with plans to expand)
● Home delivery. You can have organic food delivered to your door by an increasing number of home-delivery services or 'box' schemes, some of which supply direct from farm to home. The Soil Association provides a list (you can find their address in Part 3)
● Farm shops, health-food stores, mail-order suppliers. Check the Soil Association's list for your nearest supplier.

YOUR LEGAL RIGHTS

Labelling policies may be confusing and the science may be baffling, but the law on food shopping is relatively straightforward.

By law, shoppers have a right to expect that the food they buy shall be 'of the nature, substance and quality demanded' – note the word 'demanded'. That means that if you discover what you've bought doesn't live up to your expectations then you have a right to take it back to the shop where you bought it. Shops are responsible for the food they sell, and many supermarkets already offer a no-quibbles money-back guarantee.

Also by law, food must in theory be of satisfactory quality and be safe. GM foods must be approved before they can be grown or used in food, but now questions are being asked about who would be legally responsible if, at some time in the future, a risk to health is discovered. Who should be responsible: the farmers who grew the crops, the manufacturers who made the food, the shops which sold it, or the government which approved it?

At present it is not clear whether any of them would be legally liable – the Consumer Protection Act 1987, which makes producers legally responsible for any injury or damage caused by defective products, specifically excludes agricultural produce. Consumer organisations believe this is an unsatisfactory situation and want product liability extended to agricultural products, including GM foods.

TRADING STANDARDS

Local authorities employ Trading Standards Officers (for food labelling and standards) and Environmental Health Officers (for food hygiene and safety) to enforce consumer and food-safety laws. If you are unhappy about the way your local shops or restaurants are handling the issue of GM foods, you can talk to them. These officers are responsible for ensuring that foods and food premises are safe and that food is correctly labelled. Where breaches of the law are found, they have the powers to take companies to court.

For GM foods, Trading Standards Officers are responsible for enforcing the law, i.e.:

● The labelling of GM foods is correct
● The companies are labelling GM ingredients where they are required to
● The GM-free claims are genuine.

With product tests costing around £100 an item, there is likely to be a limit to the number of random tests that local authorities will be able to carry out.

Trading Standards and Environmental Health Officers can be contacted at or through your local Town Hall.

In Part 2, we look at which companies are providing GM-free food. Use our tables to check hundreds of everyday foods and brands.

Part 2
THE LISTINGS

Assessing the Products

We would like to have tested every single product on sale to see which ones are genuinely free of GM ingredients. This would have taken us several years, and even then we would not have been sure, as the testing procedures for some products – including those for tomato purée and derivatives such as lecithin and soya oil – have not been fully assessed yet, and would give unreliable results.

So instead we started by doing what any careful shopper does – we read the labels. Thousands of labels. We scoured the supermarkets examining products and checking the ingredients to see whether they may, possibly, contain GM material.

We also contacted the manufacturers and asked them to put their current policies and practices on GM food in writing. We asked them about GM ingredients (which have to be labelled) and about GM-derived ingredients (which don't). Then we also contacted distributors in the health-food and wholefood trades, and checked what the companies have been telling them, and we talked with campaigning and certification bodies to check out their information.

Besides our own research, we are particularly indebted to the hard work of several other groups who have been investigating the GM sources of our foods. These are:

● **The Vegetarian Society**, which is reviewing its list of approved products allowed to carry their V logo. From the summer of 1999 their logo appears only on GM-free products (i.e. products defined like our ☑ products), although their criteria does allow the use of GM chymosin for making vegetarian cheese.
● **SUMA Wholefoods**, who compile an excellent catalogue of products they distribute. The company has investigated which products are likely to be free of GM material.
● **The Essential Trading Co-operative Ltd**, which

produces a catalogue (like the SUMA catalogue) that lists products that the manufacturer has assured them are GM free.

● Organic producers and certification bodies, such as the **Soil Association**, who have worked hard to keep GM material out of our food supplies.

Our list of foods provides details of nearly 2,000 branded food products, listed under food categories from alcoholic drinks and baby foods to vinegar and yogurt. The list shows which brands are GM free ☑, which ones are questionable ?, and a few that are known to contain GM ingredients ☒.

WHAT WE LOOKED FOR

There are several food ingredients and additives that could be derived from GM crops. Some – such as cornsyrup – are clearly derived from maize, and could therefore be from GM sources. Some – such as the vitamin riboflavin (B2, used as a colouring agent as well as for fortification) – could be derived from GM bacterial sources. Unless the manufacturers could convince us that their sources were completely GM free, we have to report that they may be from GM sources.

These are the ingredients that could be genetically modified or that may be derived from GM sources

● **corn** May include GM maize
● **cornflour, cornmeal** May include cornflour from GM maize
● **corn oil** May include GM-derived maize oil
● **cornsyrup** A sugar derived from maize starch, which may include GM maize starch
● **dextrose, fructose** Sugars that can be derived from maize starch, including GM-derived maize starch
● **glucose syrup** Can be derived from maize starch, including GM-derived maize starch
● **hydrogenated vegetable oil/fat** May include soya oil,

including GM-derived soya oil

● **hydrolysed vegetable protein** May include protein from GM soya

● **maize** May include GM maize

● **maize flour** May include flour from GM maize

● **maize oil** May include GM-derived maize oil

● **maltodextrin** Can be derived from maize starch, including GM-derived maize starch

● **margarine** May include soya oil, including GM-derived soya oil

● **modified cornflour** May include cornflour from GM maize

● **modified maize flour** May include flour from GM maize

● **modified starch** May include maize starch, including GM-derived maize starch

● **riboflavin** Could be produced using GM technology

● **soya oil** May include GM-derived soya oil

● **soya protein** May include protein from GM soya

● **soya protein isolate** May include protein from GM soya

● **starch** May include maize starch, including GM-derived maize starch

● **textured vegetable protein** May include protein from GM soya

● **tomato paste, tomato purée** Could be made with GM tomatoes

● **vegetable oil, fat or suet** May include soya oil, including GM-derived soya oil

● **vegetable protein** May include soya protein, including protein from GM soya

● **vitamin B2** Another name for riboflavin – see above

● **xanthan gum** Can be derived from maize starch, possibly including GM-derived maize starch

● **yeast extract** Derived from the brewing process, where GM yeast could be used.

● **yeasts** GM yeasts for baking and brewing have been approved, but are understood not to be in widespread commercial use

Additives
The following additives may be derived from GM sources. Those in bold are more likely to be derived from GM sources, and we included these in our criteria for questioning companies about whether their products were GM free.

● **E101** and **E101a** Riboflavin, a colouring and a vitamin used to fortify some foods. The UK government's advisers approved the production of riboflavin using GM technology in 1997

● **E150** Caramel colouring, a colouring agent made from chemically treated sugar. The most common source is sugar from sugar beet and sugar cane, but sugar from maize starch may be used, in which case GM maize may provide the base material

● **E153** Carbon black, a colouring derived from burnt vegetable matter, which could include GM crops

● E160d Lycopene, a red dye derived from tomato extracts, which in theory may include GM tomatoes

● **E161c** Cryptoxanthin, a yellow dye that may be derived from maize, possibly including GM maize

● E306–9 Relatives of vitamin E that can be distilled from soya oil, possibly including oil from GM soya

● **E322** Lecithin, an emulsifier usually made from soya, possibly including GM soya

● E415 Xanthan gum, a gum derived from starch, possibly including GM maize starch

● **E471**, E472a, E473, E475, E476b, E477, E479a, E479b A range of emulsifying agents derived from animal and vegetable fats, which may include GM soya oil

● E570, E572, E573 Anti-caking agents which can be derived from fats or oils including soya oil

● E620, **E621**, E622, E623, E624, E625 A range of flavour-boosting chemicals including monosodium glutamate (E621), made by bacterial fermentation of vegetable protein such as soya protein, possibly including GM soya protein

Company Policies

THE SUPERMARKETS

The majority of UK supermarkets have recently made statements about removing GM ingredients from their own-brand foods or reducing the number of products containing them. Iceland was the first to make such a commitment in 1997 when the company said that by 1 May 1998 none of its own-brand foods would contain any GM ingredients.

More recently a number of other leading retailers – ASDA, Marks & Spencer, Sainsbury's and Waitrose – have made announcements about phasing GM ingredients out of their own-brand products, although for some companies it is not clear whether this commitment includes phasing out GM derivatives that don't need to be labelled. Other stores, such as the Co-op CWS and Budgens, say they are working towards eliminating GM ingredients from as many own-brand products as possible. None of the retailers we contacted were able to provide guarantees that animal feed used by their suppliers would be GM free, although both Iceland and Tesco have said that they are working to establish non-GM animal-feed supplies.

Where companies' own-brand products are not already completely GM free, we asked them whether they provided a list of GM products for customers. Where such lists are available they are indicated below.

If you are unsure about any of the foods in your shopping basket, contact the supermarkets direct – we've provided their addresses and phone numbers.

ASDA

ASDA told us that they have removed GM soya and maize from many of their own-brand products, including sandwich spreads, baked beans, sausages, sausage rolls, pork pies, pasties and pies. The company now has 'around 40 ASDA brand products on sale where the GM protein is present. Over the next six

53

months, it is likely that these remaining 40 or so products will also move to ingredients that are from certified non-GM sources.'

ASDA says that it will label derivatives of GM crops, such as GM-derived soya oil and lecithin, that may be present in their products.

⬤ **Contact**: ASDA Public Relations, ASDA Stores Ltd, ASDA House, Southbank, Great Wilson Street, Leeds, West Yorkshire LS11 5AD.
☎ 01132 418047. **Fax** 01132 418015.

Boots

'A small number of Boots brand products do or may contain genetically modified ingredients or their derivatives. These products will be labelled in accordance with current legislation. Sandwiches which may contain GM ingredients are still being sold without labelling or other warning.'

The company head office can provide a list of foods with GM ingredients. The company does not provide a list of own-label foods containing GM derivatives.

⬤ **Contact**: Boots The Chemist, City Gate, Nottingham NG2 3AA.
☎ 0115 950 6111. **Fax** 0115 949 5488.

Budgens

'At present Budgens does not sell products which themselves have been genetically modified, only some products containing genetically modified ingredients. A genetically modified ingredient included in some of our own-label products is genetically modified soya. We will work with our suppliers of own-label products to ensure wherever possible that no new products will contain genetically modified soya. For existing own-label products that contain GM soya we are working with our suppliers to source non-GM alternatives wherever possible.'

Budgens provides a list of 13 own-label products that contain GM soya. This includes beefburgers, quiches, sausage rolls, pork pies and fresh sandwiches. The company does not provide a list of own-label foods containing GM derivatives.

● **Contact**: Budgens plc, Stonefield Way, Ruislip, Middlesex HA4 0JR.
☎ 0181 422 9511 or their **freephone** 0800 562 002. **Fax** 0181 966 6093.

Co-op CRS
'We are not opposed in principle to selling genetically engineered food, but we do consider any moral, ethical, religious or food-safety issues. We do therefore stock genetically modified foods that are safe, legal and appropriately labelled so as to enable our customers to exercise their own choice. We have taken numerous steps to ensure we clearly label our own-branded products next to the ingredients. We cannot guarantee that branded products will be labelled, although we are encouraging all our suppliers to include this information on their labels in the same way.'

The company does not have a list of foods containing GM ingredients or derivatives sold in its stores.

● **Contact**: Co-operative CRS, Sandbrook Park, Sandbrook Way, Rochdale, Lancashire OL11 1SA.
☎ 01706 713000, or their **GM Hotline** 01706 892 183. **Fax** 01706 892 228.

Co-op CWS
'We are working with our suppliers to reduce and/or exclude the use of GM ingredients or derivatives in Co-op brand. Where this is not possible due to a lack of segregated/alternative supplies, our policy is to label these foods clearly. Our policy applies to all derivatives irrespective of whether or not modified DNA or protein is present in the finished product.

There are currently around 80 products, either on the shelf or in the pipeline, which are labelled in this way.' The company was not able to provide a timescale for these objectives. It also told us, *'The Co-op CWS is the only retailer to label many Co-op cheeses as produced using genetic modification and so suitable for vegetarians.'*

The company provides a list of Co-op brand products labelled to indicate the presence of GM ingredients. These include beefburgers, chicken dishes, ready meals, pies, pasta, biscuits, cakes, popcorn and salad dressings. The company does not provide a list of own-label foods containing GM derivatives.

● **Contact**: Co-op CWS, PO Box 53, New Century House, Manchester M60 4ES.
☎ 0161 834 1212 or their **freephone** 0800 317 827.
Fax 0161 832 2751.

Holland and Barrett

The company says that it *'can guarantee that own-label foodstuffs are free from modification'*. From September 1997 *'we de-listed any stocked product which required labelling'*. This means that the company may continue to stock products, including food supplements and remedies, that contain GM derivatives, such as lecithin or soya oil, and these may not be labelled.

● **Contact**: Holland & Barrett Retail Ltd, Samuel Ryder House, Townsend Drive, Nuneaton, Warwickshire CV11 6XW.
☎ 01202 244 400.

Iceland

'Iceland removed all GM ingredients from the Iceland brand products within our store from production 1 May 1998. We decided to remove ingredients that contained the protein/DNA from GM crops as well as derivatives that had no DNA/protein present e.g. soya oil.'

Iceland says it is now working to remove GM-derived processing aids and additives, and to establish non-GM animal-feed supplies, but that *'we are not able to provide non-GM animal-feed guarantees at present'*.

● **Contact**: Iceland Frozen Foods Ltd, Second Avenue, Deeside Industrial Estate, Deeside, Flintshire CH5 2NW.
☎ 0181 951 1313 or their **GM Hotline** 0990 133 373.

Marks & Spencer

In March 1999 Marks & Spencer announced that it would be removing all genetically modified ingredients including derivatives from St Michael food products *'as quickly as possible'*. The company could not give us a timescale.

● **Contact**: Marks & Spencer plc, Michael House, 47 Baker Street, London W1A 1DN.
☎ 0171 268 1234. **Fax** 0171 268 2777.

Safeway

Safeway told us, *'We will label all ingredients from a GM source; this includes derivatives.'*

The company says it provides a regularly updated list of products that contain GM ingredients which is available on request from any Safeway store.

● **Contact**: Safeway Stores, 6 Millington Road, Hayes, Middlesex UB3 4AY.
☎ 0181 848 8744. **Fax** 0181 573 1865.

Sainsbury's

'The work Sainsbury's has done over the past 18 months means only 40–50 products, out of 1,500, currently contain GM soya protein or DNA. These products are labelled. With Sainsbury's commitment to eliminate GM from its own-brand products, these products will be discontinued if a GM-free alternative cannot be found.' The company says it aims to have

GM soya out of products by 'the end of the summer [1999]' and that it 'will be winding down stocks of GM tomato purée ... this product will be off shelves by the end of the summer'.

'In addition Sainsbury's are working on all own-brand products which contain ingredients which could be GM derivatives, such as soya oil and lecithin. Wherever possible alternatives are being found but again if this is not possible these products will also be discontinued.' The company says it has no timescale for this.

● **Contact**: J Sainsbury Ltd, Stamford House, Stamford Street, London SE1 9LL.
☎ 0171 695 6000 or their **GM Hotline** 0500 301010.
Fax 0171 695 7610.

Somerfield
The company has asked the suppliers of its own-brand foods to source soya that is free from genetic modification. But 'where this is not possible to guarantee we have introduced clear labelling to enable the customer to make an informed choice. It is our intention to label all GM additives and to label them as soon as possible.'

The company says it provides a list of GM-free products. It will also provide on request a list of products that are GM labelled, including, in the future, products that include oil, lecithins and other additives from GM sources.

● **Contact**: Somerfield Stores, Somerfield House, Whitchurch Lane, Bristol BS14 0TJ.
☎ 0117 935 6441. **Fax** 0117 935 6015.

Tesco
The company told us, 'Since 1 September 1998 Tesco has been labelling own-brand products that contain GM ingredients and derivatives. Many Tesco products, including all fresh produce, and breads and biscuits in our bakery department, do not come from a GM source. Where we cannot guarantee that

products are free of GM products or their derivatives they will be labelled.' Tesco said it was the first supermarket to go beyond the requirements of the law and label derivatives such as oil and lecithin. It also announced in 1998 that it would be seeking to source its meat from producers who excluded GM material from animal feed.

The company says a list of GM/non GM foods is available at the information desk in stores.

● **Contact**: Tesco Corporate Affairs, Tesco House, Delamare Road, Cheshunt, Herts EN8 9SL.
☎ 01992 632 222. **Fax** 01992 646 272.

Waitrose

'Our policy is not to have GM ingredients in our own-label products from 1 April 1999. Over the past 18 months we have been progressively reformulating Waitrose own-label foods (and pet foods) to avoid the use of genetically modified soya and maize.

'We continue to work on the issues of oils, additives and other derivatives, and wherever possible our intention is to remove them as well. We are extending our labelling beyond the existing legal requirements to include additives and ingredients derived from genetically modified (GM) plants, even though the final product contains no GM materials.'

● **Contact**: Waitrose (John Lewis Partnership), Southern Industrial Area, Bracknell, Berkshire RG12 8YA.
☎ 01344 424680. **Fax** 01344 825 211.

EUROPEAN-WIDE SUPERMARKET ACTION

Marks & Spencer, Sainsbury's and five supermarket chains in continental Europe have formed a consortium to establish tracing and testing procedures in order to verify the authenticity of GM-free supplies. The five other chains are:

Carrefour (France)
Effelunga (Italy)
Migros (Switzerland)
Delhaize (Belgium)
Superquinn (Ireland)

FOOD MANUFACTURERS

We asked manufacturers the following questions:

● Do you have a statement of your company's position on GM foods?
● Do you permit GM ingredients in your brands?
● What ingredients do you label? Do you go beyond what the law requires and label derivatives such as oil and lecithin from GM sources?
● Do you produce a list of products containing GM ingredients?
● Do you produce a list of products that are GM free?
● Do you require animal feed to be GM free for products such as meat, eggs and milk?
● Do you use GM-derived riboflavin (vitamin B2)? If so, in which products?

Few companies answered all our questions, but here are extracts from company statements on their GM food policies. To find out more, contact the companies using our contacts list starting on page 177.

Aspall (cider, vinegar)
'All our products are GM free. By GM free we mean no GM-derived ingredients at all.'

Baby Organix (organic baby foods)
'We guarantee that all our products are free from GMOs because we use 100% organic ingredients ... We have signed written agreements with all our suppliers that they do not use GMOs and none of our products contain soya or soya derivatives. When we say GM free this covers all ingredients, not just those that have to be declared.'

Bart (spices)
'At the present time we prefer not to use them, or derivatives thereof ... Nevertheless ... it is becoming increasingly difficult to give absolute assurances concerning the use of GM foods or derivatives of GM crops that might apply to the food items that we produce for public consumption.'

British Bakeries (Hovis, Mothers Pride, Nimble, Granary)
'I can assure you that, at the present time, no such ingredients are included in any of our products. British Bakeries use Identify Preserved Soya (IP-Soya) from Canada. Its purity is supported by a full audit trail from seed certification through to milling.'

The company did not provide any guarantees that other ingredients, such as vegetable oil or emulsifiers, were not from GM sources.

British Sugar (Silver Spoon)
'The UK sugar beet crop, from which sugar is extracted and sold in the retail market under the Silver Spoon brand and to the food industry direct by British Sugar, has not been the subject of any genetic modification. Neither are there any plans to introduce genetically modified varieties in the foreseeable future.'

Cauldron Foods (tofu, vegetarian foods)
'Our stated aim is that we must be GM free by 31 March 1999.'
It is unclear whether this includes GM derivatives.

Chivers Hartley (jams, sauces, pickles)
'We will fully investigate the status of all ingredients used and where necessary find alternatives so that we do not use GM materials in our products. When this is not possible we currently comply with the requirements of the Labelling Regulations and are now arranging to go further than the law requires by declaring ingredients derived from GM sources. However, to date, we have found no products which would require so labelling.' The company provides a list of GM- and GM-derivative-free products.

Coca-Cola (soft drinks)
'Coca-Cola does not use any ingredient which is genetically modified.' The company were unable to clarify whether this includes ingredients that are derivatives of GM crops.

Haldane (Granose, Haldane, Releat, Dietburger)
'We have sourced, and continue to do so, all soya ingredients produced from non-genetically modified soyabeans ... we are randomly DNA-testing finished products for further reassurance.'

Heinz (soups, pasta, Weight Watchers, baby foods, Farleys, John West)
'We have ensured that ingredients used in Heinz varieties do not contain genetically modified material. In response to the concerns of many consumers and as part of our commitment to continuous improvements, we have been working very closely with our suppliers to review the use of soya- and maize-derived ingredients ... We are changing recipes to avoid their use or ensuring that we only use non-GM, identity-preserved ingredients from audited suppliers.'

Kellogg's (breakfast cereals, snacks)
'We are conscious of consumer sensitivities on this subject and avoid using genetically modified materials in our cereal products sold in Europe. For example, the maize Kellogg uses in Europe is a special variety grown in Argentina and we have specifically requested that our suppliers ensure that our maize is free of GM materials. In Kellogg grain-based morning foods, such as Nutri Grain bars, we use soya derivatives, such as soya oil, as ingredients.' The company could not guarantee that these are from non-GM soya. *'Riboflavin (B2) in Kellogg's products is not of GM-origin.'*

Linda McCartney (frozen vegetarian foods)
In February 1999, Sir Paul McCartney said: *'We at Linda McCartney Foods are strongly against genetically modified food. We wish to exclude it from our products but, despite the most stringent testing at every stage of production, a minuscule percentage may have crept through. If we, with our constant vigilance, couldn't prevent such tainting, what chance does the average person have of controlling the amount of genetically modified foods in their own lives?*

'A period of calm, during which people can decide their own future on this issue, would be extremely useful. In the meantime we are working flat out to correct any mistakes that may have occurred, in the interest of good pure food for all. We remain opposed to GM foods, and we are confident that all our products are absolutely safe or we would not release them.'

Loseley (dairy, ice cream)
'We do not use GM ingredients nor GM-derived ingredients at all.'
The company requires GM-free animal feed for animal products.

McCain Foods (frozen foods, pizza, chips)
'All ingredients used to manufacture McCain Foods (GB) products are free from GM material with the exception of some of the Humdingers range, which we currently import from the

USA. These contain either maize flour or maize starch. We are in the process of reformulating Humdingers products which do contain US sourced maize, and would anticipate being able to confirm that ALL ingredients in McCain Foods GB products are GMO free by the middle of 1999 at the latest.'

Manor Bakeries (Cadbury's cakes, Mr Kipling)
'It is not our policy to make GM-free claims or guarantees and our policy is to declare those GM ingredients which are covered by legislation.'

Mars Confectionery (confectionery, ice cream)
'We can confirm that none of our products contain any genetically modified materials.' The company did not provide reassurances that derivatives, such as vegetable fat/oil and lecithin, were from non-GM sources.

Nestlé (pasta, soups, ready meals, frozen foods, ice cream, coffee, confectionery)
'Nestlé UK does not currently sell any products requiring labelling under current GM legislation.' The company says it is currently considering how best to address the issue of derivatives.

New Zealand Milk UK Ltd (formerly Anchor)
'In saying that our products are GM free, and referring specifically to the butter and cheese ranges, we mean no GM-derived ingredients. We are concerned that there may be a degree of cross-contamination in the Anchor Aerosol cream ranges which is being urgently addressed. New Zealand Dairy cattle eat only natural New Zealand pasture, which is, by definition GM free.'

Northern Foods (Express Dairies, Eden Vale, Fox's Biscuits, Bowyers)
'Northern Foods has a positive approach towards the use of genetically modified materials in the manufacture of food

products ... *Although we do not deliberately select GM materials, the lack of segregation of GM soya and maize from non-GM materials in the commodity markets means that we cannot guarantee GM-free soya and maize in our products. We do, however, have a European source guaranteeing GM-free maize for milling.'* The company says it has no policy on use of GM materials in animal feed, nor on GM yeast, although *'we are not knowingly using GM yeast'.*

Nutricia (Cow & Gate/Milupa baby foods/drinks, diabetic foods)
'We do not and have not used any genetically modified soya or maize in our infant milks and foods.'

Plamil (soya products, dairy-free foods)
'We have established global contacts to ensure that our soya and all our products will remain non-genetically engineered.' The company says that this includes GM derivatives.

Rachel's Dairy (organic dairy foods)
'We have no GM material whatsoever in any of our product range.' This includes GM-derived ingredients.

Scottish Courage (beers and lagers)
'We do not use GM ingredients at all in our products or in the brewing process.'

JA Sharwood (sauces, spices)
'It is not our policy to make GM-free claims or guarantees and our policy is to declare those ingredients which are covered by legislation.'

Tilda Rice (rice, Madhur Jaffrey products)
'Our policy has always been one of avoiding the use of genetically modified ingredients. To the best of our knowledge, we confirm that no Tilda or Tilda & Madhur Jaffrey products contain GM materials.' The company did not indicate whether

this includes derivatives.

Unigate (dairy foods, St Ivel)
'We do not use soya protein in any St Ivel products. In line with many other UK manufacturers of food products, we are currently using in some of our products soya-based derivatives, e.g. refined soya oil and lecithin. We do not label additives or processing aids such as soya oil, lecithin or maize starch.'

Unilever (Van den Bergh, Walls, Birds Eye, Batchelors, Brook Bond)
'All products containing soya protein/flour are labelled accordingly.' All Van den Bergh Foods' margarines and spreads *'do not contain any ingredients from GM crops'.* The company says soya-derivatives may be from GM sources. The company provides a list of products containing GM ingredients.

United Biscuits (McVitie's, Ross Young's, KP, Linda McCartney)
'United Biscuits and its businesses adopted a non-GM strategy about 18 months ago. This means that, where appropriate, non-GM alternatives have been substituted for soya and maize ingredients; or if substitution is inappropriate or impossible, we source traditional, segregated crops, i.e. non-GM crops ... McVitie's (UK) is moving to a source of non-GM lecithin from Brazil ... expected to be completed by 1 April 1999.'

Weetabix (cereals, Alpen, Ready-Brek)
' ... guided by current government caution and consumer concern at this time, we find it appropriate not to use material from genetically modified crops. Any likely GM-derived enzymes or processing aids are sourced from non-GM alternatives.'

Whole Earth Foods (organic canned foods, cereals, sauces, preserves)
'None of our products contain GM ingredients.'

Yeo Valley (organic and non-organic dairy foods)
'It is our policy not to use ingredients in our products which knowingly contain GM material.' This includes GM-derived ingredients and GM processing aids. *'All milk supplied from the Yeo Valley Farms and Pedigree Lakemead Herds of dairy cows are fed with silage and or feed which has been guaranteed to be free from GM ingredients.'* The company could not provide this assurance for its non-organic milk and milk products.

A RESOUNDING SILENCE
The following companies did not provide us with the information we requested:

● **AG Barr** (Irn-Bru, Tizer)
● **Allied Bakeries** (Allison, Sunblest, Mighty White, Kingsmill, HiBran, Vitbe)
● **Bernard Matthews** (fresh and frozen meat products)
● **Burtons** (Biscuits, Wagon Wheels)
● **Cadbury** (chocolate, hot drinks, cakes, Bournvita, Bournville)
● **Campbell's** (soup, Freshbake, Fray Bentos, V-8 juice)
● **Dairy Crest** (dairy foods, spreads, Clover, Yoplait, Frijj)
● **Dalepak Foods** (frozen foods)
● **Jane Asher** (party cakes)
● **Kraft Jacobs Suchard** (Dairylea, All Gold, Birds, Angel Delight, Kenco, Kraft, Maxwell House, Toblerone, Twiglets, Vitalight)
● **MD Foods** (milk, butter, cheese, Lurpak)
● **Müller** (yogurts and desserts)
● **Pepsico** (soft drinks)
● **Quaker Oats** (cereals)
● **Schweppes** (soft drinks, Kia Ora, Sunkist)
● **SmithKline Beecham** (Ribena, Lucozade, Horlicks)

A-Z Listings

The following symbols are used in the product listings below.

☑ Means that the product is certified as organic or there are other good reasons to believe there are no GM or GM-derived ingredients. Items showing ☑ are your best bet for GM-free shopping. However, some foods showing a ☑ may have used GM-derived enzymes or processing aids, which don't have to be mentioned on the label – such as chymosin, a chemical that helps to make cheese without the need to use calves' rennet. This does not apply to organically certified foods, which should be completely GM free.

? Means that there are good reasons to believe there are no GM ingredients, but there may well be some GM-derived ingredients such as soya oil, lecithin, starch or GM-derived additives that don't have to be declared as GM-derived on the label. We list these additives. Some manufacturers and supermarkets say they will be declaring which products have GM-derived ingredients, so for items showing ? you may want to check the pack for a manufacturer's declaration, or check with the manufacturer or supermarket.

✗ Means the manufacturer acknowledges that some or all of the product range is likely to have GM ingredients. As some manufacturers are undergoing reformulations, these items may change.

Our listing has been made in good faith and the products and ingredients are described to the best of our knowledge. We apologise for any errors or omissions, and we welcome information and comments that we can incorporate into subsequent editions.

The symbols described above serve only to comment on the possible presence or otherwise of GM ingredients. They do not imply that the goods concerned have, or lack, any other characteristics whatsoever, nor should they be taken as an endorsement or otherwise of any particular brands or foods.

Abalone See Shellfish

Agar See Thickeners

☑ **Akee** (see also Tinned vegetables)

Alcohol-free and low-alcohol drinks

Unlike alcoholic drinks, alcohol-free and low-alcohol drinks have to be labelled with their ingredients. Typically, these will be similar to alcoholic drinks, plus extra flavourings and preservatives. It is understood that there is no GM yeast available for commercial brewing.

☑ Ame
☑ Aqua Libra
☑ Kaliber
☑ Tennent's LA
☐ Vita Malt (caramel colouring)

Alcoholic drinks

Food-labelling laws have for many years allowed alcoholic drinks to escape the need to list ingredients. Even when they contain GM ingredients, you have no right to know. The yeasts used for brewing may be genetically modified, as government advisers approved a GM yeast for brewing in 1994, but it is understood that this is not currently in widespread use. Only one large brewery (Scottish Courage) stated to us that they did not use GM ingredients in the brewing process. Besides yeast, the colouring agent E150 (caramel colouring) is used for many beers and some spirits. This can be derived from corn starch including GM corn starch. The development of GM yeasts for wine fermentation is under way, but it is not clear to what degree they are in use in the main wine-producing countries. There is no requirement to declare whether imported drinks have been fermented with GM yeasts.

☑ organically produced wines, beer, etc
☑ Rock's Country Wines
☐ Scottish Courage: John Smith's, Fosters, McEwan's,

Courage, Kronenbourg, Beamish, Theakston's, Newcastle Brown, Holsten, Kestrel, Youngers, Websters, Hofmeister, Molson (not using GM yeast, but ? caramel colouring)
- ☑ Vinceremos wines, beers and ciders
- ☑ Vintage Roots organic wines
- ☑ Weston's organic cider

☑ Alfalfa and alfalfa seeds
There is no GM alfalfa permitted to be sold in the UK, but GM alfalfa is being developed in the USA, primarily for cattle feed.

Almonds See Nuts

☑ **Anchovies** See Fish and Tinned fish

☑ **Apples** (see also Fruit juices, Fruit pies, Sauces and Tinned fruit)
There are no GM apples permitted to be sold in the UK, but research is being undertaken on apples resistant to blight, including an apple-pear cross, and apples with delayed ripening and decaying characteristics, allowing longer shelf lives and greater transportation of fruit.

☑ **Apricots** (see also Dried fruit and Tinned fruit)
There are no GM fresh apricots permitted to be sold in the UK, but research is being conducted into GM varieties and a GM combination of apricot and plum.

Arrowroot See Thickeners

☑ **Artichokes** (see also Tinned vegetables)

☑ **Asparagus** (see also Tinned vegetables)
There is no GM asparagus permitted to be sold in the UK, but field trials of GM asparagus are being undertaken in the USA.

☑ Aubergine
There is no GM aubergine permitted to be sold in the UK, but

71

research is being undertaken to genetically modify the aubergine to reduce the bitterness of the plant juice, and field trials are under way.

☑ **Avocado pears**

Baby foods
Tinned and dried baby foods, like many processed tinned and dried foods, contain bulking agents such as starches, which may be derived from GM maize. They may also contain vegetable oils, possibly from GM soya or maize, and the added vitamin riboflavin made using a GM process.
☑ Baby Organix
❓ Cow & Gate Olvarit (vegetable oil, cornflour)
☑ Eco-Baby
☑ Familia
❓ Farley's (vegetable oil, maltodextrin, riboflavin)
❓ Farley's Rusks (maize flour, vegetable oil, riboflavin)
❓ Heinz (vegetable oil,)
☑ Hipp Organic
❓ Milupa (maltodextrin, vegetable fat, riboflavin)

Baby fruit drinks
These are generally made from fruit syrups and water, and are therefore likely to be GM free.
☑ Cow & Gate Fruit Drinks
☑ Heinz Fruit Drinks

Baby milks and follow-on milks
Babies under six months should be drinking breast milk or an approved formula milk. According to the UK Department of Health, soya-based formula milk should be used only on medical advice. Milk-based baby drinks are subject to concerns over the feeds being given to cows and goats (see Milk, below). Cow & Gate told us that their milk powder came exclusively 'from cows fed solely on grass'.

After six months babies may start drinking follow-on milks.

These are also likely to contain unspecified vegetable oils.

☑ Baby Nat organic
☐? Cow & Gate formula (vegetable oil, soy lecithin)
☐? Cow & Gate Infasoy (glucose)
☐? Cow & Gate Step Up (vegetable oil, maltodextrin, lecithin)
☐? Farley's formula (vegetable oil, maltodextrin)
☑ Joannusmollen Eco-Lac follow-on milk
☐? Milupa Aptamil (vegetable fat)
☐? SMA Gold/White formula (vegetable oil, lecithin, riboflavin)
☐? SMA Progress (vegetable oil, lecithin, riboflavin)
☐? SMA Wysoy (soya OK if use-by date is after 2002, glucose)

☐? Bacon

Generally, bacon contains added water and curing salts. Some may contain sweetening agents, such as dextrose, which may be derived from GM sources. As with all meat products there is the possibility that the animal was fed with GM maize or soya (see Meat, below).

Bagels

Like bread, bagels are made using yeast, although it is currently unlikely that this is a GM yeast. Some of the emulsifiers used could be derived from soya.

☑ Lenders
☑ New York (☐? Blueberry bagels contain corn pieces)

Baguettes See Bread

Baked beans

The most common beans for baked beans are Navy beans, which have not been genetically modified. However, the tomato sauce can include modified starch from GM maize, and tomato purée from GM tomatoes.

☐? Heinz regular and Healthy Balance (modified cornflour)
☐? HP Baked Beans (tomato paste, modified starch, soya flour, vegetable oil)
☐? HP Beans with black pudding (tomato paste, modified starch)

? Match! HP Beans with meatballs (tomato paste, vegetable oil, dextrose, modified starch)

☑ Whole Earth

Baking ingredients (see also Cake mixes, Yeast)
There are no GM raising agents apart from yeast, and it is understood that no GM baker's yeast is used or sold commercially in the UK, although government advisers approved a GM baker's yeast in 1990. Icing sugar is GM free, and so are the sugars and most of the colours used for cake decorations (although it is possible that colouring E101 and E150 could be derived from GM sources). Chocolate for baking is likely to be made with vegetable fat and lecithin, both of which may be derived from GM soya. Flavourings and colourings may include glycerol, derived from fats and oils which might be derived from GM maize or soya.

? Betty Crocker All-Purpose Baking Mix (vegetable oil, dextrose)

? Nisa Mixed Peel (glucose syrup)

? Scotbloc cooking chocolate (vegetable oil, lecithin)

? Supercook Hundreds and Thousands (vegetable fat, glucose syrup, lecithin)

? Whitworth's Glacé Cherries (glucose syrup)

☑ **Bananas**
There are no GM fresh bananas on sale in the UK, but dried bananas may have been sweetened with glucose syrup, so check the labels (see Dried fruit). GM bananas are being developed to resist fungal attack.

Baps See Bread

Barbecue sauce See Sauces

☑ **Barley**
Barley is one of the world's main grain crops, largely used for animal feed and for brewing. There is no GM barley permitted to be sold in the UK, but research is under way to develop GM

crossbreeds of wheat and barley to create novel types of flour.
- ☑ Whitworth's Pearl Barley

Batter mixes

The simplest batter mixes consist of flour and water and a
raising agent. Some mixes come sweetened with glucose syrup,
which may be derived from GM maize.
- ❓ Golden Fry's Original Chip Shop (dried glucose syrup)
- ☑ McDougall's

Bean dishes

- ☒ Batchelors Beanfeast (GM soya)

Beans, bottled

There are no GM beans permitted to be sold in the UK, but some
beans are bottled in sauces that may contain GM-derived
ingredients.
- ❓ Green Giant Provençal Beans (tomato paste, modified starch)
- ☑ Valfrutta

Beans, dried

The only dried beans that may be genetically modified on sale in
the UK are soyabeans (see Soya, below). These should be
labelled with a GM declaration. Watch out also for mixtures of
dried beans (e.g. for soups or salads) that may include
soyabeans. If in doubt about soyabeans, buy organic versions, as
these are not permitted to be GM varieties.
- ☑ all dried beans except soya
- ☑ Essential organic beans
- ☑ organic soyabeans
- ☑ Suma organic beans

☑ **Beans, green** (see also Tinned vegetables)

Beans, tinned

As with dried beans, the only beans that may be genetically
modified and on sale in the UK are soyabeans. These should be

labelled with a GM declaration. Watch out for mixtures of beans that may include soyabeans. Watch out also for beans in sauces, where the sauce may include GM or GM-derived ingredients, including tomato purée, modified starch, glucose syrup and vegetable oil. If in doubt, buy organic versions.

- ? Old El Paso Refried Beans (vegetable oil)
- ✓ Pataks
- ✓ Suma organic tinned beans

✓ Bean sprouts

Beef See Meat

Beefburgers See Meat products

Beef extract
- ? Bovril (riboflavin)

Beer See Alcoholic drinks

✓ Beetroot
There is no GM beetroot permitted to be sold in the UK. Preserved beetroot is usually sold in vinegar, which is also not GM.
- ✓ Baxters pickled beetroot

Beverages See Alcoholic drinks, Carbonated drinks, Hot beverages, Mixers, Soft drinks and Sports foods and drinks

✓ Bilberries and blueberries

Biscuits (see also Crackers)
Biscuits typically include a range of fats, oils, starches and sugars, which can be derived from GM crops. Many also include chocolate, which in turn may include lecithin and vegetable fat, which may come from GM soya.
- ✓ all organic biscuits
- ? Burton's Chocolate Digestives (soya lecithin, vegetable oils,

glucose syrup)
- ? Cadbury's Time Out (vegetable fat, dextrose, soya lecithin, maize starch)
- ✓ Doves Farm organic
- ? Fox's Crinkle Crunch (vegetable oils, glucose syrup, lecithin)
- ✓ Glutano gluten-free
- ✓ Granny Anne gluten-free
- ✓ Horizon (Maryland)
- ✓ Kallo organic
- ✓ McVitie's: Penguin, Rich Tea, Digestives, Go-Ahead, Jaffa Cakes, Hobnobs
- ✓ Prewetts Carob
- ? Wagon Wheels (glucose syrup, vegetable oil, soya lecithin)
- ✓ Whole Earth cookies

✓ **Blackberries** (see also Tinned fruit)

✓ **Blackcurrants** (see also Tinned fruit)
There are no GM blackcurrants permitted to be sold in the UK, but genetic-modification research on blackcurrant promoter genes has been undertaken by the makers of Ribena.

? Black pudding
This is a type of sausage made using blood, fat and seasonings. As with all animal products, GM maize and soya may have been used in animal feed. Organically produced animals are not permitted to be fed with GM feed. Other ingredients that may be found in savoury puddings and sausages include vegetable fats, soya protein and soya flour, and modified starch, all of which may be derived from GM crops.
- ? HP Beans with black pudding (tomato paste, modified starch)

? Blini
These are a type of pancake traditionally made with buckwheat. Those that use oils and sweetening ingredients may be using oil or glucose syrup from GM sources.

Bloaters See Smoked fish

☑ **Bran**
Pure bran is the husk of wheat (or sometimes oat) grains, and no GM wheat or oats are permitted to be sold in the UK.
☑ Herons wheat bran
☑ Mornflake oat bran
☑ Suma organic oat, wheat brans

Brazil nuts See Nuts

Breadcrumbs
Much of the commentary for bread also applies to breadcrumbs, although some breadcrumbs are prepared without fat.
☑ Goldenfry Golden Breadcrumbs

Bread, rolls, baps, etc
Bread and similar products made from dough are likely to include fats and oils that could be derived from GM sources, and they may use soya flour and lecithin emulsifier, both of which could be derived from GM soyabeans. In addition, UK government advisers approved the commercial use of a GM yeast in 1990, although this yeast is understood not to be in widespread use at present. British Bakeries told us they were not using GM yeasts in their products.
☐? Allied Bakeries: Kingsmill, Allinson, Day Fresh, Mighty White, Sunblest (soya flour, vegetable fat, emulsifiers)
☑ all organic breads and rolls
☑ Barkat rice breads
☐? British Bakeries: Mothers Pride, Hovis, Nimble (vegetable oils, emulsifiers)
☑ Clara's Kitchen bread mixes
☑ Cranks
☑ Eghoyan's wholemeal pitta
☑ Eurobuns burger buns
☑ Glutano gluten-free
☐? Goswell's (vegetable oil)

? Heinz Weight Watchers (glucose syrup)
✓ House of Westphata Rye Bread
✓ La Fornia seed bread, organic bread
✓ Maharaji Naan bread
? Nisa frozen cheese baguettes (vegetable oil)
✓ Pataks Naan bread
✓ Suma Naan bread
? Sun Maid Raisin Loaf (vegetable fat, soya flour, dextrose)
✓ Sunnyvale organic
? Vogel's (vegetable oil)
? Warburton's Milk Roll (vegetable fat, soya flour)

Breakfast cereals (see also Muesli, Bran, Wheatgerm and individual cereals)
Many breakfast cereals include corn (maize), some include vegetable fat, and many are fortified with vitamin B2 (riboflavin). All of these ingredients can potentially be derived from GM processes.
✓ Doves Farm organic
✓ Familia organic
✓ GranoVita organic
✓ Grapenuts
? Heinz Weight Watchers (maltodextrin, riboflavin)
✓ Jordans organic
✓ Kallo
✓ Kellogg's: Corn Flakes, Rice Crispies, All Bran, Frosties, etc.
✓ Mornflake Crunchy, Crisp and oat products
✓ Nature's Path organic
? Nestlé brands with starch, glucose syrup, vegetable oil, riboflavin
✓ Nestlé Shredded Wheat
✓ Quaker Oats (but ? Oatso Simple contains lecithin)
✓ Scott's Porage Oats
✓ Suma oats
✓ Weetabix: Advantage, Bran Flakes, Corn Flakes, Weetabix, Ready-Brek
✓ Whole Earth organic

☑ **Broccoli**

Brownies See Cakes and Cake mixes

☑ **Brussels sprouts**
There are no GM Brussels sprouts permitted to be sold in the UK, but the development of GM sprouts, cabbage and spring greens resistant to pests is under way.

☑ **Buck wheat**
Not strictly a cereal but treated as such, it is a staple food in areas of Asia.

Bulgur wheat or Burghul wheat See Wheat

❓ **Buns**
Like breads and cakes, commercially made buns are likely to contain vegetable fats, soya flour, emulsifiers and sweetening agents such as glucose syrup, all of which might be derived from GM sources. Buns raised with yeast could use a GM yeast that UK government advisers approved for commercial use in 1990, although it is understood that this yeast is not in widespread use at present.
❓ Sunblest Hot Cross Buns (vegetable fat, emulsifiers, modified starch)

❓ **Burger buns** (see also Bread)
These have similar ingredients to bread, plus a sesame-seed coating. There are no GM sesame seeds permitted to be sold in the UK (see Sesame, below).

Burgers See Meat products and Vegetarian products

Butter See Fats and oils

☑ **Cabbage**
There is no GM cabbage permitted to be sold in the UK, but the

development of GM sprouts, cabbage and spring greens
resistant to pests is under way.

Cake mixes

Cake mixes are typically made with starches, sweetening agents
and vegetable fats and oils that could be derived from GM
sources. They may also use soya flour and lecithin emulsifier,
both of which could be derived from GM soyabeans.

[?] Betty Crocker Cake Mix, Brownie Mix (vegetable oil, dextrose,
maize starch, maltodextrin, riboflavin)

[?] Greens cake mixes (vegetable oil, maize starch, maltodextrin,
glucose syrup, cornflour)

[?] Shake-a-Cake (soya lecithin, vegetable oil, modified starch,
soya flour)

Cakes

Cakes are likely to be made with fats and oils that could be
derived from GM sources, and they may use soya flour and
lecithin emulsifier, both of which could be derived from GM
soyabeans.

[✔] Bakery Henk Keune organic

[✔] Biona organic honeycake

[?] Cadbury's Mini Rolls (vegetable fat, lecithin, glucose syrup,
dextrose, soya flour)

[?] Cadbury's frozen cakes and gateaux (vegetable fat, glucose
syrup, dextrose, lecithin, modified starch)

[✔] De Rit organic honeycake

[✔] McVitie's Go-Ahead frozen gateaux

[?] Mr Kipling Frozen Slices (vegetable oil, glucose syrup,
dextrose, soya flour)

[?] Mr Kipling Cake Bites, Fruit Cake (vegetable oil, lecithin,
glucose syrup, xanthan gum, soya flour, dextrose, modified
starch)

[?] Mrs Crimble's Dutch Loaf (cornsyrup)

[✔] Respect Organic Carrot Cake

[✔] Saker organic cakes

[?] Sara Lee frozen gateaux (vegetable oil, modified starch,

glucose syrup, lecithin, soya flour)
- ☑ Sunnyvale organic
- ☑ Village Bakery organic cakes

Calamari See Squid

Callaloo See Tinned vegetables

Candied peel
The fruit content is likely to be GM free, but the sugars may include glucose syrup, which can be derived from maize, including GM maize.
- ☑ La Bio-Idea organic
- ? Nisa Mixed Peel (glucose syrup)
- ? Whitworth's Glacé Cherries (glucose syrup)

Canned products See Tinned

Canola oil (rapeseed oil) See Fats and oils

☑ **Capers**

Capsicums See Peppers

Carbonated drinks (see also Mixers and Sports foods and drinks)
Care has to be taken with carbonated drinks as they come in different sizes and formats (glass and plastic bottles, cans) and more importantly in different formulations. A canned version may use sugar as a sweetening agent, while a bottled version may use glucose, which may be derived from GM maize. Some drinks also contain a colouring agent, E150 (caramel colouring), which can be derived from sugar or from glucose, including GM-derived glucose.
- ? Canada Dry (caramel colouring)
- ? Cherry Coke (caramel colouring)
- ? Coca-Cola (caramel colouring)
- ? Dr Pepper (caramel colouring)

- ☑ Fanta
- ☑ Fentiman's ginger beer, lemonade
- ☑ Free cola, lemonade, etc
- ☑ Gusto
- [?] Idris Ginger Beer (glucose syrup, modified starch)
- ☑ Irn-Bru
- ☑ Lilt
- [?] Lucozade (glucose syrup)
- ☑ Orangina
- [?] Pepsi, Pepsi Max (caramel colouring)
- ☑ Power Rangers
- ☑ Purdey's
- [?] Red Bull (glucose, caramel colouring)
- ☑ Rio Tropical
- [?] R Whites Lemonade (glucose syrup)
- [?] Schweppes Ginger Ale (caramel colouring)
- ☑ Selzer
- ☑ 7-Up
- ☑ Sprite
- [?] Tango (fructose and glucose in bottled versions)
- ☑ Thorncroft
- ☑ Tizer
- [?] Vimto (glucose, fructose)
- [?] Virgin Cola (caramel colouring)
- ☑ Whole Earth cola, lemonade

Carrageenan See Thickeners

☑ **Carrots** (see also Tinned vegetables)
There are no GM fresh carrots permitted to be sold in the UK, but both American and Japanese researchers are undertaking field trials of GM carrot varieties with greater disease resistance and with altered nutritional qualities.

☑ **Cassava**

Cat food See Pet food

☑ Cauliflower

There is no GM fresh cauliflower permitted to be sold in the UK, but field trials of GM cauliflowers developed for greater frost resistance are being undertaken in the USA.

Caviar (see also Roe)
☑ Marina lumpfish caviar

☑ Celeriac

☑ Celery

There is no GM fresh celery permitted to be sold in the UK, but field trails of GM celery are being undertaken in the USA.

Cereal bars
Like many baked products, cereal bars may be sweetened with sugars that can be derived from maize, including GM maize. They may also contain maize or soya oil, including oil from GM maize or soya.
☑ Doves Farm flapjacks
☑ Essential organic flapjacks
☑ Jordans Crunchy bars and apricot-almond Frusli bar
❓ Kellogg's Nutri Grain (glucose syrup, vegetable oil, maltodextrin, lecithin, modified starch, riboflavin)
☑ Lyme Regis flapjacks
❓ Mars Tracker (glucose syrup, vegetable fat, lecithin)
❓ Quaker Harvest (glucose syrup, cornsyrup, vegetable oil, riboflavin)
☑ RJ Foods flapjacks
❓ Sesame Snaps (glucose syrup)
☑ Wholebake flapjacks and cereal bars

Cereals (see also Breakfast cereals, Flour, Barley, Maize, Millet, Oats, Rice, Rye, Sorghum and Wheat)
Cereals form the largest sector of basic staple foods in the world, used for both human food and farm-animal feeds. Considerable research is going into the genetic modification of

cereal crops to increase their resistance to pests and increase their yield. No GM cereals are permitted for sale in the UK apart from maize (see Maize, below).

☑ all plain cereal products (e.g. rolled oats, wholewheat flakes, barley and millet flakes) apart from maize

☑ organically grown maize

Chapatti
? Patak (vegetable oil, lecithin)

Cheese
There are three GM concerns with cheese. The first is whether the milk used for the cheese was produced using the milk-boosting hormone bovine somatotropin (BST), made with genetic-engineering technology (see Milk, below). BST is not being used for UK or European Union dairy herds, but cheese produced in the USA may have been made from BST-boosted milk.

The second concern is whether the cheese was made using a genetically engineered version of an enzyme called chymosin. Some shoppers take the view that GM chymosin represents a good use of GM technology as it avoids the need to use rennet, the traditional cheese-making enzyme extracted from calves' stomachs. Many manufacturers use GM chymosin, which was first given government approval in 1991, but only the Co-op's own-brand cheese has declared it on the label. Some manufacturers refer to cheese made with GM chymosin as vegetarian cheese, although it is increasingly used in regular cheesemaking. Certified organic cheese is made using a more expensive non-GM, non-animal version of chymosin.

The third aspect of cheese production, and the production of eggs, meat and other animal products, is whether the animal was fed GM feed. Both maize and soya are common ingredients of animal feedstuffs. Very few cheesemakers ask the milk suppliers what they fed to their livestock, so it can be assumed that most mass-produced cheese will be made from milk supplies that include milk from GM-fed animals. The main exception to this is for food produced organically, as organic dairy herds should not be fed GM-produced material.

☑ all organically certified cheeses

? all other European Union-produced cheese (GM feed, chymosin). These include all the common cheeses found in the supermarkets: Brie, Camembert, Caerphilly, Cheddar, Cheshire, cottage cheese, Edam, Gouda, Leicester, Lancashire, soft cheeses (e.g. Boursin, Philadelphia), Stilton, etc

? United States-produced cheese (BST, GM feed, chymosin). We get few US cheeses in the UK, although we get some cheese products (see Cheese spreads, below)

Cheesecakes

Like cake mixes, these can contain GM-derived starches and sugars, and lecithin emulsifiers. They may also use cheese or cheese powder made using GM chymosin (see Cheese, above).

? Birds Cheesecake Mix (vegetable oils, modified starch, cheese powder, soya lecithin, xanthan gum)

? Heinz Weight Watchers frozen cheesecake (vegetable oil, glucose syrup, modified cornflour, margarine, lecithin)

Cheese spreads and processed cheese

Cheese spreads and processed cheeses generally take a cheese and blend it with milk or water and an emulsifier. The same comments apply to processed cheeses as apply to cheese (see Cheese, above) regarding BST and chymosin.

? Cheestrings (EU-produced cheese)

? Dairylea (EU-produced cheese, modified starch)

? Kraft Cheddarie (EU-produced cheese)

? Kraft cheese slices (EU-produced cheese)

? Kraft Cracker Barrel Spreadable (EU-produced cheese)

? Laughing Cow (EU-produced cheese)

? Old El Paso Cheese Salsa (sauce containing US-produced cheese)

? Old Fashioned Foods Squeeze Cheese (US-produced)

? Philadelphia (EU-produced cheese)

? Primula (EU-produced cheese)

? Primula Light (EU-produced cheese)

Cheese substitutes

These use vegetable-based ingredients to replace the milk in cheese. Some are based on soya or use vegetable oils, both of which may be from GM crops (see Soya, below).

? Flora Alternative to Cheddar (vegetable oil)

✔ Cherries (see also Tinned fruit)

Cherries are GM free, but glacé cherries may be prepared in glucose syrup, which can be derived from maize, including GM maize.

? Whitworth's Glacé Cherries (glucose syrup)

✔ Chestnuts

Chestnuts are GM free but chestnut products may be thickened or sweetened with starches and sugars that can be derived from maize, including GM maize.

✔ Porter's unsweetened purée

Chewing gum and bubble gum

These products may include sweeteners such as glucose syrup derived from GM maize, and lecithin from GM soya.

? Hollywood (glucose syrup, lecithin)

? Hubba Bubba (glucose syrup, lecithin)

✔ Wrigley's Orbit, Extra

? Wrigley's Spearmint, Doublemint, Juicy Fruit, PK (dextrose, glucose syrup, modified starch)

Chicken and turkey (see also Meat products)

No GM chicken is permitted to be sold in the UK, but recently reported genetic manipulations showed the possibility of producing chickens with legs in place of wings. As with other farm animals, chickens, turkeys and other farm poultry receive feeds that often include maize and soya, and this may include GM maize and soya (see Meat, below). Poultry reared under organic certification schemes are not fed with GM products. Self-basting chickens may include vegetable oils, which might be derived from maize or soya, including GM maize or soya, as well as dextrose and lecithin, which might come from GM maize and soya respectively.

☑ organically reared chickens and other poultry

? Bernard Matthews Sliced Turkey Breast (?feed, caramel colouring, dextrose)

? Bernard Matthews Wafer Thin Turkey Ham (?feed, starch, dextrose)

? Birds Eye frozen Chicken Chargrills (?feed, vegetable oil, modified starch)

? Gott's Cooked Chilled Roast Chicken (?feed, caramel colouring, corn starch, dextrose)

? Mattesson's Turkey Rashers (?feed, dextrose)

Chicken nuggets See Meat products

Chickpeas See Beans

☑ Chicory

There is no GM fresh chicory permitted to be sold in the UK, but herbicide-resistant chicory has been developed and is permitted to be grown for research purposes in the European Union, including the UK. GM varieties of chicory are permitted in food in other parts of the world. Preparations from chicory may contain sweetening or thickening agents derived from GM sources – check the ingredients on the label.

☑ Prewetts Chicory Drink

Chilled meals See Ready meals

Chillies See Peppers

Chinese-style food (see also Noodles and Sauces)

Like most ready meals and dishes, Chinese-style foods tend to contain the common ingredients of modified starch and glucose syrup, both of which may be derived from GM maize. Chinese dishes also favour the use of soy sauce (see Sauces) and soyabeans, both of which may be from GM crops. In addition, some dishes may use GM tomato paste.

? Amoy Soy Sauce (soya)

? Amoy Stir-Fry sauces (modified starch, soyabean oil, soy sauce, hydrolysed vegetable protein, soyabeans, caramel colouring, tomato paste)

? Birds Eye Chicken and Black Bean Sauce (soyabeans)

✔ Blue Dragon oriental foods

✘ Daloon's Spring Rolls (maize starch, vegetable oil, GM textured soya flour, soy sauce)

? Emperor's Palace frozen sweet and sour sauce (modified starch, tomato paste, soy sauce, vegetable oil)

? Joe Smokes Chinese frozen pork ribs (modified starch, glucose syrup, tomato paste, soy sauce, E150)

? Oriental Express frozen spring rolls (vegetable oil, cornflour, dextrose, monosodium glutamate)

✘ Sharwood's Black Bean Stir-in Sauce (GM soya)

? Sharwood's Stir-Fry Sauces (modified cornstarch, sweetcorn, vegetable oil, tomato paste, soy sauce, soyabeans)

? Uncle Ben's Stir Fry Sauce (vegetable oil, modified starch, soy sauce, caramel colouring, lecithin)

? Wing Yip Chinese sauces (corn starch, soya protein, vegetable oil)

? Wok (Oriental Express) frozen dishes (tomato paste, modified starch, soy sauce, dextrose)

Chips and frozen potato products

The potatoes in chips are not genetically modified (see Potatoes, below), although there are developments to create a GM potato with reduced starch, allowing it to be deep fried without absorbing as much fat. The oils for frying potato products may well be soya or maize oil, which could be from GM sources. Some products are also coated with a sprinkling of starch or dextrose that may be from GM maize, and monosodium glutamate, which may be from GM soya.

✘ Birds Eye Crunchy Jacks (vegetable, oil, GM soya protein)

? Birds Eye Potato Waffles (vegetable oil, starch)

✔ Greenacres potato products

[?] Hula Hoops frozen rings (vegetable oil, maize starch, monosodium glutamate)
[x] McCain's Humdinger products (can contain GM starch, being reformulated by mid-1999)
[✔] McCain's Oven Fries, Home Fries, Microchips
[✔] Young's Chip Shop Chips

Chocolate and confectionery (for hot chocolate see Hot beverages)

Chocolate may be made with added vegetable fat, including soya, which may come from GM sources. It usually uses soya lecithin as an emulsifier. Confectionery may also use starches and sugars, such as glucose syrup, which may have been derived from GM maize.

[?] Bassett's Licorice Allsorts (glucose syrup, modified starch, cornflour)
[?] Boots Shapers, Crispy Caramel Bar (lecithin, vegetable oil)
[?] Cadbury's chocolate bars, Boost, Roses (vegetable fat, lecithin, glucose syrup)
[✔] Elite chocolate bars
[✔] Equal Exchange chocolate Brazils
[✔] Essential carob-coated nuts and raisins
[✔] GranoVita bars
[✔] Green & Blacks Organic chocolate products
[✔] Grizzly bars
[?] Kellogg's Rice Krispies Squares (glucose syrup, fructose, vegetable oils, riboflavin)
[?] Mars Bars, Bounty, Galaxy, Maltesers, M&Ms, Snickers, Starburst, Topic, Twix (vegetable fat, glucose syrup, lecithin, modified starch, dextrin)
[✔] Molle Skovly chocolates, chocolate nuts, nougat
[?] Nestlé Rowntree Aero, Rolo, Pastilles, Toffee Crisp, Milky Bar, After Eight, Smarties, Kit Kat, Polo Mints (modified starch, glucose syrup, lecithin, vegetable fat, E101)
[✔] Oxfam Mascao chocolate bars
[?] Payne's Poppets (glucose syrup, lecithin, modified starch)
[✔] Plamil carob, chocolate bars

☑ Shepherdboy bars
☑ Sweet Temptation gluten-free confectionery
❓ Terry's plain chocolate, Chocolate Orange (lecithin)
☑ Traidcraft chocolate nuts, raisins, chocolate bars
☑ Trebor Cool Mints
❓ Werther's Originals (glucose syrup, lecithin)

Chocolate spread (see also Nut spreads)
❓ Kruger chocolate spread (vegetable oil, lecithin)
❓ Nutella (vegetable oils, lecithin)
☑ Stute Hazelnut and chocolate spread

Christmas pudding See Desserts (for brandy sauce see Sauces)

Chutneys
Vegetables and fruit, vinegar and sugar form the basis of a chutney, and all of these should be GM free in the UK. Watch out for thickening agents such as modified starch, and sweetening agents such as glucose.
☑ Oxfam Swazi Kitchen Chutneys
❓ Rajah Chutneys (modified starch)
❓ Sharwoods Green Label Mango Chutney (glucose syrup)

Cider See Alcoholic drinks

☑ **Cocoa** (see also Hot beverages)
Cocoa is GM free, but check the ingredients list to be sure the manufacturer has not added any hidden extras, such as lecithin or vegetable fat.
☑ Cadbury's cocoa
☑ Equal Exchange organic cocoa
☑ Green & Black organic cocoa
☑ Hambledon Herbs organic cocoa

☑ **Coconut**
There is no GM coconut permitted to be sold in the UK. Coconut

derivatives such as desiccated coconut and coconut cream and milk are usually free of added extras, but check the label to be sure.

☑ Best-In Creamed Coconut
☑ Dunn's River Coconut Milk
☑ Essential organic coconut
☑ Nisa desiccated coconut
☑ Prima desiccated coconut

☑ **Cod** (see also Fish)
Frozen cod products are described in Fish products, below. Cod is rarely tinned but may be salted, in which case the usual only added ingredient is salt.
☑ Dunn's River Salted Cod

☑ **Coffee**
There is no GM coffee permitted to be sold in the UK, although there is research into creating a GM coffee been that is caffeine free. For now, pure coffee beans and instant coffee powder and granules are GM free. Coffee mixtures such as instant cappucino may have added ingredients such as those found in coffee creamers (see below).
☑ Café Direct
☑ Camp Essence
☑ Clipper Organic
☑ Douwe Egbert
☑ Equal Exchange organic
☑ Kenco
☑ Lyons
☑ Nescafé
☑ Suma
☑ Symington's Dandelion Coffee
☑ Traidcraft
☑ Whole Earth NOCAF, Wake Cup

Coffee creamers
These substitutes for milk may include vegetable fat, glucose syrup or colouring, all of which might be derived from GM crops.

? Kenco (glucose syrup, vegetable oil)
? Nestlé Coffeemate (vegetable oil, glucose syrup, riboflavin)

Coleslaw

This is a mixture of vegetables (cabbage, carrots, onion, etc) with a mayonnaise-style dressing. The vegetables will be GM free but the dressing may include vegetable oils, glucose syrup and xanthan gum, which may be derived from GM crops.

? Mattesson's coleslaw (vegetable oil, xanthan gum)

☑ **Coley** See Fish

Cones and wafers

Like biscuits, wafers may use soya flour, lecithin and other possibly GM-derived ingredients.

? Askey Pompadour wafers (lecithin)
☑ Glutano gluten-free wafers
? Marcantonio Cones (lecithin)
☑ Rivingtons wafers

Confectionery See Chocolate and confectionery

Convenience food See Ready meals

Cooking fats See Fats and oils

Cook-in sauces See Sauces

Cordials See Soft drinks

☑ **Coriander** (see also Herbs and spices)

Corn See Maize, Popcorn

Corned beef See Meat products

Cornflour See Thickeners

☑ **Courgettes**

☑ **Couscous**
Couscous is made from wheat (see Wheat, below), and no GM wheat is permitted for sale in the UK, but ready-to-eat salads made from couscous may include vegetable oils derived from maize or soya, including GM maize or soya.
❓ Delphi Couscous Salad (vegetable oil)

Crab and crabsticks See Shellfish

Crackers (see also Biscuits, Crispbread and Crisps)
Like sweet biscuits, savoury crackers may include various ingredients that could be derived from GM sources.
❓ Carr's Water Biscuits (vegetable oils)
☑ Fortt's Original Bath Olivers
☑ Kallo rice crackers
☑ McVitie's TUC Cheese Crackers
☑ Rakusen's crackers and matzos
❓ Ritz Crackers (vegetable oil)

☑ **Cranberries** (see also Sauces, Fruit juices and Tinned fruit)
There are no GM cranberries permitted to be sold in the UK, but field trials of GM cranberries are being undertaken in the USA.

Cream and cream substitutes
There are several concerns about the use of GM processes in the production of milk and milk products. For more on this, see Milk, below. For food produced organically, dairy herds should not be fed GM-produced material. Cream substitutes rely on vegetable fats and emulsifiers that may be derived from GM maize or soya crops.
☑ all organically produced dairy foods
☑ Anchor Dairy Cream Spray
❓ Delissimo (Anchor) (emulsifiers, glucose syrup)
❓ Elmlea Cream Substitute (vegetable oil, lecithin)
❓ Marvel (GM feed, glucose syrup)

☑ Nestlé Simply Double (vegetable oil, maltodextrin)
☑ Rachel's Dairy cream and buttermilk
☑ Yeo Valley organic cream, crème fraîche

Crème fraîche See Cream

Crispbread (see also Crackers and Biscuits)
☑ Orgran gluten-free
☑ Ryvita (except ? Ryvita Multigrain includes kibbled soya)

Crisps and bag snacks
Makers of crisps and bag snacks tend to shop around for their ingredients, and may change the sources of their starch and their vegetable oils according to price and availability.
☑ Apache tortilla chips
? Boots Shapers crisps (vegetable oil)
☑ Clearspring rice crackers
☑ Essential Bombay mix, rice crackers, etc
? Go-Ahead Crinklins (starch, vegetable oil, glucose syrup)
☑ Golden Wonder Wheat Crunchies salt & vinegar/spicy tomato/worcester sauce flavours
? Golden Wonder other products (modified starch, vegetable oil, maize)
☑ Jordans cheese/tomato chips
☑ Kettle crisps in sunflower oil
? KP Skips, Hula Hoops (maize, vegetable oil)
☑ McVitie's Mini Cheddars
☑ Mexi Snax tortillas
? Pringles (vegetable oil, cornflour, modified starch)
☑ Stamp vegetable chips
☑ Trafo organic crisps
? Twiglets (vegetable oils, soya lecithin)
? Walkers Crisps, Doritos, Quavers (vegetable oil, soya flour)

? Croissants
Like breads and cakes, croissants may include vegetable fats, soya flour, emulsifiers, and sweetening agents such as glucose,

all of which might be derived from GM sources. Croissants raised with yeast may use a GM yeast approved by government advisers in 1990 for commercial use, but it is understood that this yeast is not yet in widespread use.

? Croutons
Like bread, croutons may include vegetable fats, soya flour and emulsifiers, which might be derived from GM sources.

? Crumpets
Like bread, crumpets are likely to be raised with yeast, which could be GM yeast although it is understood that GM baker's yeast is not in widespread use at present. They may also include sweetening or browning agents such as dextrose or glucose, which might be derived from GM maize.
? Sunblest crumpets (dextrose)

✔ Cucumbers
There are no GM cucumbers permitted to be sold in the UK, but research is under way into creating GM salad vegetables with greater resistance to pests, greater tolerance of pesticide sprays, and slower decaying properties giving them a longer shelf life and greater transportation potential.

Currants See Dried fruit

Curries See Ready meals, Sauces and Herbs and spices

Curry powder See Herbs and spices

Custard (see also Milk puddings)
Originally, custard was a sauce based on eggs and milk, but nowadays it is more likely to consist of milk thickened with cornflour (which may be from GM maize flour) and coloured yellow with dyes. There are several concerns about the use of GM processes in the production of milk and milk products, including the use of a GM milk-boosting hormone called bovine

somatotropin, and questions about the contents of the animal feed used for the cattle. For more on this, see Milk, below.

? Ambrosia Devon Custard (modified starch)

? Birds Instant Custard Powder (modified starch, vegetable oil)

? Farmlea Custard (dextrose)

Dairy spreads See Fats and oils

☑ **Damsons**

Dates See Dried fruit

Dessert mixes and toppings
Typical dessert mixes include thickening agents, fats and sweetening agents, blended with emulsifiers and colourings. These ingredients can be derived from soya and maize, including GM soya and maize.

? Angel Delight (maltodextrin, vegetable oil, modified starch, lecithin)

? Atora Suet Pudding Mix (vegetable oils)

? Birds Dream Topping, Instant Whip, Trifle Mix (vegetable oil, maltodextrin, lecithin, modified starch, cornflour)

? Birds frozen Superwhip (vegetable oil, glucose syrup, lecithin)

? Green's Carmelle Dessert Mix (glucose syrup, caramelised syrup)

? Nestlé Tip Top (modified starch, vegetable fat, lecithin)

☑ Silver Spoon Treat topping

Desserts, frozen (see also Cakes and Ice Cream)
Like frozen cakes and pastries, frozen desserts are likely to include a range of thickening and sweetening agents and vegetable fat, and these ingredients may be derived from soya or maize, including GM soya or maize.

? Aunt Bessie's frozen Spotted Dick (vegetable fat)

? Sara Lee Danish, Raspberry Rhapsody, Lemon Meringue (modified starch, vegetable oil, glucose syrup, soya flour, lecithin, dextrose)

? Walls Vienetta (vegetable fat, glucose syrup, lecithin)

Desserts, ready-to-eat (see also Jelly, Milk puddings and Yogurt and fromage frais)
Chilled, ready-to-eat desserts can include thickening and sweetening agents that may be derived from maize or soya, including GM maize or soya. These desserts may also include milk (see Milk, below).
? Cadbury's Chocolate and Cream Trifles (vegetable fat, chocolate chips, modified maize starch, maltodextrin)
? Cadbury's Mousse, Monty Mousse, Flake Dessert (vegetable fat, modified maize starch)
☑ GranoVita soya dessert
☑ Imagine vegan desserts
☑ Kallo rice pudding
? Müller Fruit Corner, Crunch Corner (dextrose, fructose, glucose, maize, chocolate)
? Müller Rice (modified starch)
? Munch Bunch Fromage Frais and Yogurts (starch)
☑ Plamil rice pudding, soya desserts
☑ ProSoya soya-yogurt
☑ Provamil tofu-yogurt
☑ Shape creamy rice
? Shape Mousse and Fromage Frais (fructose, modified starch)
? Skane Dairy Madal (vegetable oil)
☑ So Good soya yogurts
☑ Yeo Valley fruit yogurts
? Yoplait Petits Filous and Fromage Frais (glucose syrup, modified starch)

Desserts to heat
☑ Ceres Christmas Pudding
☑ Sunnyvale plum pudding

Dhal See Lentils and dhal

Diabetic foods
These may be formulated as their regular counterparts but with some or all of the sugar replaced with bulk sweetening agents

such as sorbitol, or with artificial sweeteners. They may also have reduced fat, which may be replaced with thickening agents or gums derived from maize, including GM maize. Otherwise, the same general ingredients would be expected – such as vegetable oil, starch, lecithin and fructose in biscuit products, all of which might be derived from GM sources.

? Boots diabetic biscuits (vegetable oil, fructose, lecithin)
☑ Stute Diabetic jams, marmalades

Dips (see also Hummus, Sauces and Taramasalata)
These are mixtures similar to salad dressings and mayonnaise, with additional vegetable purées. They are likely to contain oil and to be thickened with starches or gums, and these ingredients can be derived from maize or soya, including GM maize or soya. Some may also include tomato paste (see Tomatoes, below).

? Delphi Guacamole dip (vegetable oil)
? Doritos (tomato paste, modified starch)
☑ Meridian Salsa
? Old El Paso Salsa (tomato paste)
? Phileas Fogg Salsa (tomato paste)
? Primula dips (vegetable oil, modified starch, xanthan gum, tomato paste)
? St Ivel (vegetable oil, xanthan gum)

Dog food See Pet food

Doughnuts and pastries
Doughnuts and pastries are likely to be made with fats and oils that could be derived from GM sources, and they may use soya flour and lecithin emulsifier, both of which could be derived from GM soyabeans. They may also use yeast, and UK government advisers approved the commercial use of a GM yeast in 1990, although this yeast is understood not to be in widespread use at present. The filling of doughnuts and pastries may include jams and fruit fillings thickened with starches and sweetened with sugars derived from maize, including GM maize, or they may be

filled with cream or artificial cream (see Cream and cream substitutes, above).

[?] Country Style frozen jam/cream doughnuts (glucose syrup, vegetable oils, cornflour)

[?] Sara Lee Frozen Danish, Apple/Pecan (modified starch, vegetable oil, glucose syrup, soya flour, lecithin)

Dressings See Salad dressings

Dried fruit
Generally, dried fruit is treated with a preservative such as sulphur dioxide and may be moistened with a vegetable oil, which may include oils derived from GM soya or maize. Organic producers are not permitted to use GM oils.

- [✓] Allos banana chips
- [✓] Crazy Jack's organic raisins, sultanas, currants
- [✓] Essential dried fruits, loose and pre-packed
- [✓] Suma organic
- [✓] Tropical Wholefoods dried fruit

Dripping See Fats and oils

Ducks and geese
There are no GM ducks or geese. It is possible, however, that these birds may have been fed with GM soya or maize (see Meat, below). Organically produced ducks and geese are not permitted to be fed with any GM material.

Dumplings
Dumplings are a mixture of flour and fat, and the fat may be derived from soya or maize, which might include GM sources.

- [?] Atora Dumpling Mix (vegetable oils)
- [?] McDougall's Dumpling Mix (vegetable oils)
- [?] Original Farmhouse Dumpling Mix (vegetable oils)

[✓] Eels
Eels are GM free. Jellied eels usually come in a sauce made

using gelatine, but if other thickening agents are used, such as starch or gum, then it is possible these may have been derived from GM maize.

Eggs

The main concern about eggs, as with all animal products, relates to the feed given to the animals. As we discuss in the section on Meat, below, large amounts of GM maize and soya are included in animal feed in the UK, and there is some evidence that fragments of modified DNA can pass across the gut wall into the animal's organs. It is not certain if these fragments can be taken up into the eggs before they are laid, and it may prove to be the case that they are not. Organically produced eggs are required to come from hens that have not been fed with any GM material.

☑ organically produced eggs
❓ all other eggs (?feed materials)

☑ Endive

Energy drinks See Sports foods and drinks

Extracts See Beef extract and Yeast extract

Fats and oils

OILS

Olive, Rapeseed, Corn, Peanut, Sunflower, Canola, Safflower and Grapeseed

The only GM-derived oils permitted to be sold in the UK are maize and soya oils. No other oils should be derived from GM sources. Organically produced maize and soya oils are not permitted to come from GM maize or soya crops. Rapeseed (canola) crops that have been genetically modified to resist being sprayed with herbicides are being experimentally grown in the UK but none of their products should be entering the food supply. Oils from other crops undergoing trials in other parts of the world, such as GM sunflower with altered fat profiles and GM peanuts resistant to viral attack, also should not be entering the UK food supply. Bottles labelled simply 'vegetable' oil may contain blends of oils, including maize and soya, which might be derived from GM maize or soya crops.

- ☑ Clearspring sesame
- ☑ Community Foods groundnut, sunflower
- ? Crisp 'n' Dry (vegetable oil)
- ☑ Essential organic oils
- ☑ Flora sunflower
- ☑ Fry Light sprays
- ☑ Golden Fields rapeseed
- ? Mazola corn
- ☑ Meridian olive, sesame, sunflower, etc
- ? Olivio (vegetable oil)
- ? Pura Light Touch (lecithin)
- ☑ Suma olive, sesame, sunflower, etc
- ☑ Sunita organic olive

COOKING FATS

Suet, Vegetable suet, Lard and Dripping

Suet is derived from the fatty deposits around cattle kidneys, lard from pig fat, and dripping from beef fat (similar to tallow), and for all these fats there is evidence that modified gene fragments from GM maize and soya used in feed can pass across from animal feed into animal organs. The rendering process used to extract the fat from the animal may well remove or destroy much of the DNA, so that animal-based cooking fats will be virtually free of any detectable GM material. To avoid all derivatives from animals fed with GM maize or soya, then look for organic alternatives, as organically produced animals must not be fed GM material.

Vegetable cooking fats may indicate on the pack which type of fat or oil they are made from, which means they could include maize or soya, including GM maize or soya.

- ? Atora Suet (?feed)
- ? Atora Vegetable Suet (vegetable fat)

BUTTER, DAIRY SPREADS, MARGARINES
AND LOW-FAT SPREADS

Regarding butter and dairy spreads, there are several concerns
about the use of GM processes in the production of milk and milk
products. For more on this, see the section on Milk. The main
exception to this is for food produced organically, as organic
regulations state that dairy herds should not be fed GM-produced
material.

Margarines include blends of oils from vegetable and fish
sources. The fish will not include farmed fish or GM fish.
Vegetable oils, unless specified in the ingredients list, may well
include maize or soya oils, and these might be derived from GM
maize or soya. These products also use emulsifiers such as
soya-based lecithin, which may be derived from GM soya.

☑ Anchor So Soft
? Blue Band (vegetable oils, lecithin)
? Clover (vegetable oils)
? Delight (vegetable oil)
? Flora (vegetable oils, lecithin)
? Golden Churn (vegetable oils, lecithin)
☑ Granose
☑ GranoVita
? Lurpak Spreadable (vegetable oil)
☑ organically produced butter
? other butter (?feed)
☑ Rachel's Dairy butter
? St Ivel Gold (vegetable oils, modified starch)
? Stork (vegetable oils, lecithin)
☑ Suma margarines and spreads
? Summer County (vegetable oil, lecithin)
? Utterly Butterly (vegetable oil, lecithin)
? Vitalite (vegetable oil, lecithin)
☑ Whole Earth sunflower spread

☑ **Fennel**

Figs See Dried fruit

✅ **Fish** (see also Fish fingers and fish products, Shellfish, Squid and Tinned fish)

No genetically modified fish are permitted for sale in the UK. Farmed fish, such as salmon and trout, are the subject of considerable genetic research to develop breeds that grow more rapidly. An additional concern with farmed fish such as trout and salmon is the feed being given to farm-reared fish, which may include meat derivatives from animals that are in turn fed maize or soya, including GM maize or soya. 'Surimi' is reconstituted fish flakes made into solid pieces, with added flavouring (which may include monosodium glutamate, which can be derived from GM soya).

Fish cakes See Fish fingers and fish products

Fish fingers and fish products (see also Shellfish and Squid)

Boil-in-the-bag cod in sauce may contain thickeners or emulsifiers derived from GM maize or soya.

❌ Birds Eye fish fingers in batter (GM soya flour)

❓ Birds Eye fish grills, other fish fingers, fish cakes (vegetable oil, maize starch)

❓ Coldwater's Scary Sharks, Fish Bites (maize flour starch, soya flour, vegetable oil, dextrose)

❓ Young's Fish in Sauce (modified starch, margarine)

Fizzy drinks See Carbonated drinks

Flans See Cakes, Fruit pies and Quiche

Flapjacks See Cereal bars

Flavouring agents See Baking ingredients and Vanilla

Flour (see also Cereals and Thickeners)

Regular flour is made from wheat, and no GM wheat is permitted to be sold in the UK. Self-raising flour includes chemical raising agents, and these are not derived from GM technology. Flour blends, such as blends for rye bread-making, or grain-mixed flour, such as granary, could include maize – read the ingredients list to check.

- ☑ Allinson
- ☑ Allinson's Organic
- ☑ Doves Farm
- ☑ Essential
- ☑ Homepride
- ☑ Marriages
- ☑ McDougall's
- ☑ Spillers Elephant Chupatty and Elephant Naan flour
- ☑ Watermill organic

Fortified drinks See Sports foods and drinks

Frankfurters
Like sausages (see Meat products) these include a blend of meat and starches or flours. The meat may be derived from animals – typically pork or chicken – which could have been reared on GM maize or soya feed (see Meat, below). Animals reared under organic certification schemes are not permitted to be fed with GM material. The starches may be from maize, which could include GM maize. There may be extra fats or oils from vegetable sources, such as maize or soya, including GM maize or soya. The flavour may be boosted with hydrolysed vegetable protein or monosodium glutamate, both of which may be derived from GM sources.

- ☑ all organically certified meat products
- ❓ Crosse & Blackwell 'Herta' (?feed)
- ❓ Herta hot dogs in roll (dextrose, vegetable oils, modified starch, tomato paste)
- ❓ Tivall vegetarian frankfurters (soya protein, vegetable oil, starch, xanthan gum, riboflavin)
- ❓ Ye Olde Oak American Hot Dogs (?feed, starch, vegetable protein)

Fromage frais See Yogurt and fromage frais

105

Frozen desserts See Desserts

Frozen fish See Fish and Fish fingers

Frozen meals See Ready meals

Frozen meat See Meat and Meat products

Frozen vegetables (see also Chips and frozen potato products)
Most packs of frozen vegetables contain no other ingredients
besides the vegetables, and there are no GM vegetables
permitted for sale in the UK. The sweetcorn varieties are
understood not to be the GM maize permitted for sale in the UK,
so sweetcorn is, for the moment, GM free in the UK. Check the
ingredients lists on mixed-vegetable or vegetable-and-sauce
packs just in case they include unexpected ingredients such as
soyabeans, vegetable oils, starches or sweeteners that could be
derived from soya or maize, including GM soya or maize.
☑ organic frozen vegetables (e.g. Nutana)
☑ virtually all regular frozen vegetables, e.g. Birds Eye.

☑ **Fruit** (see also Tinned fruit and individual fruits)
There are no GM fruits permitted for sale in the UK. Fruit that is
packed in syrups may include glucose syrup, which might be
derived from GM maize.
☑ Dole Fruit Tubs

Fruit juices and fruit drinks (see also Juices and
Soft drinks)
Fruit juices should be pure fruit and, as there is no GM fruit
permitted for sale in the UK, all fruit juices should be GM free.
However, a technicality in the law allows manufacturers of fruit
juices to top up the sugar in pure juices to agreed 'average'
levels, and it is possible that companies are using fructose or
other sugars that can be derived from maize, including GM
maize, to do this. They are not required to declare this practice
on the label.

FROZEN DESSERTS – FRUIT JUICES AND FRUIT DRINKS

- ☑ all organic fruit juices
- ☑ Aspall fruit juices
- ☑ Community Foods apple concentrate
- ☑ Copella apple juices
- ☑ Crones organic juices
- ❓ Del Monte (?added sugars)
- ☑ Ekoland fruit concentrates
- ☑ Essential Trading fruit juices
- ☑ Jif concentrated lemon, lime juices
- ❓ Just Juice (?added sugars)
- ☑ Meridian fruit concentrates
- ☑ Stute fruit juices
- ☑ Suma fruit concentrates
- ☑ Vitalia organic juices
- ☑ Western Isle fruit concentrates
- ☑ Whole Earth aloe-lemon/tropical treat

Fruit drinks, whole-fruit drinks, fruit nectars and similar products are not pure fruit (indeed they may have as little as 5% fruit content) but are a blend of fruit juice with sweetened water and may include other flavouring ingredients and artificial sweeteners. The main concern from the GM viewpoint is the presence of sweeteners, such as glucose syrup and fructose, which may have come from GM maize.

- ☑ Ame
- ☑ Aqua Libra
- ☑ Calypso Rugrats
- ☑ Capri Sun
- ☑ Five Alive
- ☑ Flintstones Calypso
- ☑ Fruit Burst
- ❓ Libby's 'C' (glucose syrup)
- ☑ Oasis
- ❓ Sanatogen Start Up (riboflavin)
- ❓ Sunny Delight (vegetable oil, modified starch, xanthan gum)
- ❓ Um Bongo (glucose syrup)
- ❓ Vimto in carton (glucose, fructose)

Fruit pies (see also Pastry)
Pies consist of a pastry shell and a fruit-sauce filling. Pastry may include vegetable oils derived from GM sources (see Pastry, below) and the fillings may be thickened with starches and sweetened with sugars derived from maize, including GM maize.
? Freshbake (vegetable oil, modified starch, soya flour, dextrose)
? Mr Kipling's Apple Pie (vegetable oil, dextrose, glucose syrup, modified starch)

☑ Fungi
Edible fungi are GM free. Commercial mushrooms may be grown using chicken manure, which may come from chickens that have been fed maize or soya, which might in turn come from GM sources, but little of this will remain on the mushroom when eaten.

? Game
Game – wild animals such as deer, hare and rabbits, and birds such as pheasant and partridge – may be bred in captivity before being released for hunting. As with most captive animals, they are likely to be fed with a diet including maize or soya, and this might include GM maize or soya.

Garlic
There is no GM fresh garlic permitted to be sold in the UK, but research is being undertaken on developing GM strains of garlic resistant to the yellow dwarf virus. Some garlic paste is made with unspecified vegetable oil.
? Gia garlic purée (vegetable oil)
☑ Very Lazy chopped garlic

Garlic bread
Bread and similar products made from dough are likely to include fats and oils which could be derived from GM sources, and they may use soya flour and lecithin emulsifier, both of which could be derived from GM soyabeans. In addition, UK government advisers

approved the commercial use of a GM yeast for baking in 1990, although this yeast is understood not to be in widespread use at present.

? Nisa frozen garlic bread (vegetable oil)

? Speedibake frozen garlic bread (vegetable oil, soya flour, dextrose)

Gateaux See Cakes and Desserts

? Gelatine

Gelatine is a thickener and gelling agent derived from the skin, bones and connective tissue of cattle and pigs. As with all animal products, there is a possibility that the animal was fed with GM maize or soya crops. Gelatine is processed at high temperatures and using strong alkalis, and it is unlikely that any genetic material would remain detectable in the protein in gelatine.

Ghee

Ghee is made from butter or from vegetable fat. For the links between genetic modification and butter products, see Butter, above, and for the links with vegetable oils see Fats and oils, above.

? Khanum Vegetable Ghee (vegetable oil)

? Lakes Butter Ghee (see Butter)

? Plough Butter Ghee (see Butter)

Gherkins See Pickles

Ginger

There is no GM ginger permitted to be sold in the UK. Crystalline ginger may be packed in sugar solutions that include glucose syrup or other sweeteners derived from maize starch, which might include GM maize starch.

Gluten-free food

Some individuals prefer to avoid foods containing gluten, a protein found in wheat, rye, barley and, to a lesser extent, oats.

Gluten-free cereal foods rely largely on maize and rice as their main ingredient. The maize may be from GM crops. Organically produced gluten-free foods are not permitted to use GM maize.

☑ Glutano biscuits, pasta, bread, crackers, flour mixes
☑ Gluten Free Company products
☑ Granny Anne gluten-free
☑ Orgran Gourmet pasta
☑ Sweet Temptation gluten-free confectionery

Goat See Meat

Goose See Ducks and geese

☑ **Gooseberries** (see also Tinned fruit)

☑ **Grapefruit** (see also Tinned fruit)
There are no GM grapefruit permitted to be sold in the UK, but research is being undertaken on modifying the genes responsible for resisting citrus virus attack.

☑ **Grapes** (see also Tinned fruit)
There are no GM grapes permitted to be sold in the UK, but research is being undertaken to develop GM strains with increased yields, and to manipulate grape virus genes.

Gravy and stocks (see also Sauces and Yeast extract)
Commercial gravy powder, essences and stock cubes consist of thickeners and strong flavouring elements plus salt or similar flavour boosters. A common flavour booster is hydrolysed vegetable protein and another is monosodium glutamate, both of which may be derived from soya protein, including GM soya protein. The thickening agents may include starches and gums derived from maize, including GM maize. Many products also include a colouring agent, caramel colouring (E150), which is derived from sugars and these might include sugars from GM maize.
☐? Bovril stock cubes (starch, caramel colouring, maltodextrin)

? Bisto gravy granules/powder (vegetable oil, starch, caramel colouring)

☑ Bisto Garlic and Herb gravy mix, Best Onion Gravy, Vegetarian Gravy

? Goldenfry Rich 'n' Meaty Gravy Granules (vegetable oil, caramel colouring, glucose, hydrolysed vegetable protein, lecithin)

☑ Kallo vegetable stock cubes, organic liquid seasoning

? Knorr stock cubes (vegetable oils, corn starch, soy sauce, caramel colouring, riboflavin)

? Maggi stock cubes (vegetable oil, caramel colouring)

☑ Marigold bouillon

? Oxo Cubes (caramel colouring, glucose syrup)

? Oxo granules (soya lecithin, glucose syrup solids, vegetable oil)

☑ Rapunzel stock cubes

? Supercook Gravy Mix (cornflour, caramel colouring, hydrolysed vegetable protein)

? Vecon vegetable stock paste (hydrolysed vegetable protein, riboflavin)

☑ **Greengages** (see also Tinned fruit)

Grouse See Game

Guacamole See Dips

☑ **Guava** (see also Tinned fruit)

Haddock See Fish and Smoked fish

Haggis

Haggis is made from sheep offal mixed with suet and oatmeal, onions and seasoning. The meat content raises various questions about GM animal feed (see Meat, below). Vegetarian versions may rely on soya protein, soya oils and colourings derived from maize glucose, and in all these cases GM versions of soya or maize may be used.

☑ Macsween vegetarian haggis

? McIntosh vegetarian haggis (vegetable oil, caramel colouring)

? Hall's (?feed)

Halibut See Fish

Halva See Sesame

Ham (see also Meat products and Tinned meats)
The concerns with ham are similar to those for bacon (see Bacon, above). They include the addition of starches and sugars that may be derived from maize, including GM maize, and the rearing of the animals using GM maize or soya animal feeds (see also Meat, below).

? Bernard Matthews Wafer Thin Turkey Ham (?feed, starch, dextrose)

Hamburgers See Meat products

Hare See Game

? **Hash browns**
These are potato products (see Chips and frozen potato products, above) made with flour and oil. The flour may include maize flour and the oil may be derived from maize or soya, and in both cases these may include GM crops.

Hazelnuts See Nuts

Heart See Meat

☑ **Hempseed**

Herbal and fruit teas and herbal drinks
There are no GM herbs or spices permitted to be sold in the UK, and so any plain products of herbs and spices should be GM free. Products with added sweetening agents or thickeners may

include derivatives of maize, including GM maize.

☑ Ame fruit/herbal drink
☑ Aqua Libra fruit/herbal drink
☑ Bottle Green fruit/herbal cordials
☑ Celestial Seasons herbal/fruit teas
☑ Dr Stuart's herbal/fruit teas
☑ Eleven O'Clock Rooibosch
☑ Golden Temple herbal/fruit teas
☑ Hambledon Herbs organic herbal/fruit teas
☑ Heath & Heather herbal/fruit teas
☑ Herbal Garden herbal teas
☑ London Herb & Spice Company herbal/fruit teas
☑ Milford herbal/fruit teas
☑ Norfolk Punch fruit/herbal drink
☑ Rock's fruit/herbal organic cordials
☑ Thorncroft fruit/herbal cordials
☑ Twinings herbal/fruit teas

Herbs and spices

Single herbs or spices should be GM free in the UK as no GM herbs or GM spices are permitted for sale in the country. Some spice blends, however, may include flavour boosters such as hydrolysed vegetable protein or monosodium glutamate, both of which can be derived from soya, including GM soya.

☑ Barts
☑ Dunn's River Barbecue Seasoning
☑ Essential
☑ Green Cuisine
☑ Hambledon
❓ Map's All-purpose seasoning mix (monosodium glutamate)
☑ Map's single herbs and spices
❓ Rajah All-purpose seasoning mix (monosodium glutamate)
☑ Rajah single herbs and spices
☑ Schwarz
❓ Tex's Fried Chicken seasoning mix (monosodium glutamate)

Herring See Fish

Honey

Honey is produced by bees, which rely on sources of food that may include pollen and plant sugars from GM crops grown in the vicinity of the hive, and on sugars provided by the beekeeper, which might include glucose syrups and other sugars derived from maize starch, including GM maize. As much of the honey sold in the UK has been imported from countries where the rules on GM crops are different from those in the UK, it is possible that some honeys contain GM pollen fragments. Even in the UK, bees within range of the test sites for experimental GM crops could pick up GM pollen. The definitions for organic honey include a wide margin between the hive and the nearest known GM crops, and indeed between the hive and any crops treated with pesticides and other non-organic farm chemicals.

- ✔ Equal Exchange organic
- ✔ Essential organic
- ❓ Gale's
- ✔ GFM organic
- ✔ New Zealand Natural Food Company organic honey and honeycomb
- ✔ Suma wildflower
- ✔ Tropical Forest organic

Hot beverages (see also Cocoa, Coffee, Herbal teas and Tea)

These instant powdered drinks may be sweetened with glucose syrups derived from maize, including GM maize, and contain fats derived from maize or oil, including GM crops.

- ✔ Barley Cup
- ❓ Bournvita (glucose syrup, riboflavin)
- ✔ Cadbury's Drinking Chocolate
- ❓ Cadbury's High Lights (dried glucose syrup, vegetable oil)
- ✔ Equal Exchange cocoa
- ✔ Green & Black's Organic Hot Chocolate Drink
- ❓ Horlicks (vegetable fat, riboflavin)
- ❓ Maltissimo (vegetable fat, riboflavin)
- ❓ Options (glucose syrup)
- ❓ Ovaltine (vegetable fat, riboflavin)
- ✔ Prewetts Chicory Drink

☑ Symington's Dandelion Coffee
☑ Whole Earth NOCAF, Wake Cup

Hot cross buns See Buns

Hot dogs See Frankfurters

Hummus

Hummus is normally a blend of chickpea paste and sesame-seed paste, oil and flavouring ingredients. Neither GM chickpeas nor GM sesame are permitted to be sold in the UK, but commercial hummus may include unspecified vegetable oils, possibly derived from GM maize or soya. Some hummus may also be thickened with starches, which might be derived from GM maize.

☑ Cypressa
❓ Delphi Houmous (vegetable oil)
❓ Lava/Zorba (vegetable oil)
☑ Mediterranean Foods
☑ Suma
☑ Whole Earth organic

Ice creams

Ice creams are typically made with a blend of dairy fats and cheaper vegetable fats. The vegetable fats may be derived from soya or maize, which might include GM soya and maize. In addition, there are several concerns about the use of GM processes in the production of milk and milk products. For more on this, see the section on Milk, below.

❓ Ben and Jerry's (varieties with chocolate pieces may include lecithin)
❓ Häagen-Dazs (some varieties include cornsyrup, and the chocolate pieces may include lecithin)
☑ Loseley ice creams
❓ Mars Snickers, Twix, Mars Bars (glucose syrup, lecithin, vegetable oil)
❓ Walls Vienetta, Cornish, Magnum (vegetable fat, glucose syrup, lecithin)

Ice lollies

Like soft drinks, which they closely resemble, ice lollies are a mixture of sugar and water with added fruit-flavouring agents and colouring. The sweetening agents used may include glucose syrup or other sugars that can be derived from maize, including GM maize.

☑ Cadiso Lollie Mix
❓ Calypso Flintstones Freeze Pops (dextrose)
☑ Lyons Maid Mr Men
☑ Mr Freeze ice sticks
❓ Nestlé Bug Pops, Zoom, Fruit Pastil (glucose syrup, vegetable fat, xanthan gum)
❓ Walls Feast (glucose syrup, vegetable fat, lecithin)

Instant meals See Ready meals

Jams and conserves

The fruit in jams should be GM free as no GM fruit is permitted to be sold in the UK. The sweetening agents may include syrups such as glucose syrup and dextrose that can be derived from maize, including GM maize.

☑ Bionova organic jams
☑ Bonne Maman jams and marmalade
❓ Duerr's (glucose syrup)
☑ Essential organic fruit spreads
☑ Hartleys jam and marmalade
☑ Martlet fruit spreads
☑ Meridian Organic Fruit Spread, Breakfast Spread
☑ Moorhouse jams
☑ Oxfam Swazi Kitchen marmalade
❓ Robertsons Golden Shred marmalade (glucose syrup)
☑ Roses marmalades
☑ Stute
☑ Stute Diabetic
☑ Suma fruit spreads
☑ Thursday Cottage jams
☑ Whole Earth marmalades and fruit spreads

Jelly (see also Thickeners for gelatine, agar, etc)
Like soft drinks and ice lollies, jellies are a mixture of sugar and
water, flavoured and coloured, and thickened with gelatine. The
sweetening agents may include glucose syrup or other sugars
that can be derived from maize starch, including GM maize
starch. The gelatine may come from animals fed with GM maize
or soya (see Thickeners, below).
- ? Chivers Jelly cubes (?feed, glucose syrup)
- ? Green's Quick-Jel powder (?feed, modified starch
- ✔ Just Wholefoods jelly powder/crystals
- ? Rowntrees Jelly cubes (?feed, glucose syrup)
- ? Rowntrees Jelly powder (?feed, maltodextrin)
- ? Rowntrees ready-to-eat jelly (?feed)

Juice drinks See Fruit juices and fruit drinks

Juices (see also Fruit juices)
Like fruit juices, most pure vegetable juices should be free of GM
ingredients, as no GM vegetables are permitted to be sold in the
UK.
- ✔ all pure vegetable juices
- ✔ Biona carrot, vegetable juices
- ✔ Biota vegetable juices
- ✔ Eden Organic carrot juice
- ✔ Essential Trading vegetable juices
- ✔ La Verja tomato juice
- ✔ organic tomato juices
- ✔ Stelle carrot juice
- ✔ V-8 vegetable juice
- ✔ Vitalia carrot, vegetable juices

Kebabs
These consist of a shell made from pitta bread (see Bread,
above) and a filling including vegetables and meat (see Meat,
below). The main concerns are the presence of flavour-boosting
agents such as hydrolysed vegetable protein and monosodium
glutamate, which may be derived from soya, including GM soya,

and the use of GM crops for animal feed for the meat content.
? Glendale frozen Kebabs (?feed, rusk, soya concentrate,
hydrolysed vegetable protein, tomato paste)

Ketchup See Sauces

Kidney See Meat

Kippers See Smoked fish

☑ Kiwi fruit
There are no GM kiwi fruit permitted to be sold in the UK, but
field trials of GM kiwis are being undertaken elsewhere in the
world.

☑ Kumquats

☑ Lady's fingers (okra)

Lamb See Meat

Lard See Fats and oils

Latkes
Latkes are potato-based pancakes with flour and possibly oil. No
GM potato is permitted to be sold in the UK and the flour is
normally wheat flour. The oil may be vegetable oil, in which case
it may be derived from maize or soya, including GM maize or
soya.
☑ Telma latkes

☑ Leeks

Lemonade See Soft drinks and Carbonated drinks

☑ Lemons and limes
There are no GM lemons or limes permitted to be sold in the UK,

but research is being undertaken on modifying the genes responsible for resisting citrus virus attack. Concentrates of lemon and lime juice tend to be made without added sweetening agent or thickening agent.

☑ Jif concentrated lemon, lime juices
☑ Opie's preserved lemon slices

Lemon squash See Soft drinks

☑ Lentils and dhal
These are pulses that are normally sold dried and unprocessed. If processed they may be cooked with vegetable oil and thickened with starches, and these oils and starches may be derived from maize or soya, including GM maize or soya.

☑ Crazy Jacks organic lentils
☑ Essential Organic lentils and pulses
☑ Suma organic lentils and pulses

☑ Lettuce
No GM varieties of lettuce are permitted to be sold in the UK, but research is being undertaken on manipulating the genes to allow lettuce to tolerate sub-freezing temperatures and on creating GM salad vegetables with greater resistance to pests, greater tolerance of pesticide sprays, and slower decaying properties giving them a longer shelf life and greater transportation potential.

☑ Linseed

Liver See Meat

Liver sausage See Pâté

Lobster See Shellfish

☑ Loganberries (see also Tinned fruit)

Lollies See Chocolate and confectionery and Ice lollies

Low-alcohol drinks See Alcohol-free and low-alcohol drinks

Low-fat spreads See Fats and oils

Luncheon meat See Tinned meat

☑ **Lychee** (litchi)

☑ **Mackerel** (see also Smoked fish)

Maize (see also Popcorn)
A variety of maize that has been genetically modified to be resistant to pests is permitted to be marketed and used in the UK. The maize was approved by UK government advisers in 1996 and may be grown in European member states, as well as in Japan, the USA and Canada. Other GM maize varieties, including some that can withstand being sprayed by various herbicides, have been approved for growing in Japan, the USA and Canada, but not the EU. Some 40% of the US maize crop is now GM maize. Research is under way on the use of genes from grasses and other plants to develop varieties of maize that do not need to reproduce through pollination.

The products of maize find their way into a wide variety of foods and are also used in animal feeds. Little or no segregation of the GM maize crop has occurred, and manufacturers using maize derivatives are finding it hard to trace the source and to ensure that derivatives are from GM-free maize. GM maize is not permitted in organically certified products, or to be fed to organically reared animals.
☑ Aurora polenta
☑ Biosun polenta
☑ organically produced maize

Malt loaf
Like breads and cakes, malt loaf may include vegetable fats,

glucose syrup, soya flour, lecithin and other emulsifiers, and the colouring agent caramel (E150), all of which could be derived from GM sources. For malt loaves raised with yeast, UK government advisers approved the commercial use of a GM yeast in 1990, but it is understood that this yeast is not in widespread use.

☑ Lincolnshire Plum Loaf
☑ Soreen
❓ Sunmalt (soya flour, caramel colouring)

☑ Mangetout

☑ Mangoes

Margarine See Fats and oils

Marmalade See Jams and conserves

Marmite See Yeast extract

☑ Marrow

Marshmallows

These are confections of sugars and starches that could be derived from maize, including GM maize.
❓ Kidd's New York Marshmallows (glucose syrup, starch, dextrose)

Marzipan

A mixture of almonds and sugar. The sugar may include glucose syrup or other sugars that can be derived from maize, including GM maize.

☑ De Rit honey marzipan
☑ Molle Skovly organic marzipan

Mayonnaise

Mayonnaise is a blend of oil with egg and flavoured with vinegar or lemon juice. Some commercial mayonnaise products use thickening agents. The oils used may include maize or soya oil, including GM versions, and the starches, gums and emulsifiers used may be derived from GM maize or soya.

☑ GranoVita
[?] Hellmanns and Hellmanns Light (vegetable oil, modified starch, xanthan gum)
☑ Meridian organic
☑ Plamil egg-free

Meat

Although various genetically modified animals have been developed in research laboratories, none of these have been approved for commercial production for the UK food supply.

However, both soya and maize are in widespread use in animal feed in the UK, and this may easily include GM soya and maize. Other animal fodder crops that are being genetically modified include alfalfa, clover and sorghum, but these are not permitted into the UK at present. Various additives derived from GM technology are being tested for animal feed, such as enzymes that can boost the conversion of animal feed into muscle growth on pigs and calves.

Although biotechnologists may have assumed that genetically modified DNA would not pass from the animal feed into the animal's tissue, recent experiments have shown that recognisable fragments of modified genes have been detected passing from the gut into the bloodstream and from there into various organs in test animals, including spleen and placenta, and the modified DNA has been taken up into the DNA structure of white blood cells. There is no indication that the modified genes are causing health problems, but equally there is no reason to be complacent about the potential for modified genes in animal feed to pass into the human food chain.

☑ Organically reared animals are not permitted to be fed any GM ingredients in their rations

Meat extracts

These consist of meat (see Meat, above) and yeast extract (see Yeast extract, below), and may include thickening agents derived from maize, including GM maize.

? Bovril (corn starch, riboflavin)

Meat pastes See Pâtés

Meat pies (see also Pastry)

Meat pies have a pastry shell and sauce filling. The pastry is a mix including flour and fat, usually vegetable fat, which may be derived from soya or maize, including GM soya or maize. The flour is usually wheat flour, but may be blended with soya and/or maize flours, including those from GM sources. The sauce may include thickening, colouring and emulsifying agents that can be derived from soya and maize, including GM soya and maize.

☒ Bowyers frozen pork pies (vegetable oil, GM soya grits)

? Fray Bentos tinned steak & kidney pudding/pie (rusk, caramel colouring)

? Fray Bentos tinned chicken and mushroom pie (margarine, vegetable oil, maize starch)

? Freshbake frozen meat pies and pasties (vegetable oil, modified starch, tomato paste, caramel colouring, monosodium glutamate)

? Peters meat pies and pasties (margarine, modified maize starch, soya flour, caramel colouring, hydrolysed vegetable protein, soyabean oil, rusk)

☑ Proper Cornish vegetarian pastie

? Tyne Brand tinned mince pie (vegetable fat, soya protein isolate, modified starch, caramel colouring)

? Walls Chicken Slice (vegetable oils, tomato paste, modified starch, lecithin)

Meat products, chilled and frozen

Meat products start with a meat ingredient (see Meat, above) and then add a series of other ingredients including extra fat and water, held in place with emulsifiers and thickeners, colouring agents, and coating such as breadcrumb or batter, and bulking flours such as soya flour or bread rusk. All these ingredients may include products from maize or soya, including GM maize or soya. Some products also boost their flavour with yeast extract (see Yeast extract, below) or with hydrolysed vegetable protein or monosodium glutamate, both of which may be derived from soya, including GM soya.

[?] Adams sausages (rusk)

[?] Bernard Matthews Golden Drummers, Dinosaurs (breadcrumbs, vegetable oil, starch)

[?] Bernard Matthews Dinosaur turkey roll (dextrose, starch, soya protein isolate)

[✔] Bernard Matthews Lamb Roast

[?] Bernard Matthews Mini Kievs (vegetable oil, starch)

[?] Birds Eye Chicken Chargrills (vegetable oil, modified starch)

[?] Birds Eye Chicken Curry, Chicken Supreme (tomato paste, vegetable oil, modified maize starch, xanthan gum, maltodextrin, margarine and soyabeans in Chicken and Black Bean sauce)

[✗] Birds Eye beefburgers (GM soya)

[✗] Birds Eye Megaburgers (GM soy protein)

[?] Birds Eye Mighty Grill Steaks (rusk, dextrose)

[?] Birds Eye Chicken Chargrills (modified starch, vegetable oil)

[?] Birds Eye Chicken Dippers (vegetable oil, rusk)

[?] Birds Eye Chicken Lattice (margarine, vegetable oil, modified maize starch, xanthan gum)

[?] Birds Eye Chicken Marinade (vegetable oil, modified starch)

[?] Birds Eye Crispy Chicken (cornflour)

[✗] Birds Eye Crispy Chicken Strips (GM soya flour)

[?] Birds Eye Roast Beef in Gravy (maize starch, tomato paste, xanthan gum, monosodium glutamate, E153)

[✗] Buxted Looney Tunes Bites (rusk, vegetable oil, breadcrumbs, maize flour, GM modified maize starch in some versions)

[?] Campbell's American Diner Chicken Burgers (maize flour, vegetable oil, hydrolysed vegetable protein, dextrose, soya flour)

[?] Dalepak Beef Grills, Lamb Grills, Dalesteaks (dextrose, maltodextrose, corn starch, vegetable oil, hydrolysed vegetable protein)

[✗] Dalepak Chicago Ribs (includes GM soya ingredients)

[?] Feldhaus Tom and Jerry pork and chicken slice (rusk)

[?] Freshbake Glasgow frozen sausages (rusk, dextrose)

? Glendale frozen kebabs (rusk, soya concentrate, hydrolysed vegetable protein, tomato paste)

? Hall's Wee Willie Winkies (rusk, dextrose)

☑ Mattesson's Garlic/ Pork Sausage

? Mr Brain's Pork Faggotts (modified starch, tomato paste, caramel colouring)

? Perkins Premier Chicken Nuggets (breadcrumbs, vegetable oil, soya protein concentrate, dextrose, modified starch, hydrolysed vegetable protein)

? Richmond sausages (rusk, starch, soya protein)

☒ Ross Beef Grillsteaks (GM textured soya, dextrose)

? Sun Valley Chicken Kiev (breadcrumbs, vegetable oil, isolated soya protein)

? Twizzlers (rusk, vegetable oil, tomato powder, starch, dextrose)

? Walls sausages (rusk, soya protein, dextrose)

Meat substitutes See Vegetarian products

☑ Melon and watermelon

There are no GM melons permitted for sale in the UK, but research into creating GM melons and watermelons with slower ripening and decaying times is under way, and this will allow longer shelf lives and greater transportation potential.

☑ Melon seeds

There are no GM melon seeds permitted for sale in the UK. Dried roasted seeds may have salt added and, if used in a mixture of roasted, seasoned ingredients, the mix may include flavour boosters like hydrolysed vegetable protein or monosodium glutamate, both of which can be derived from soya, including GM soya.

Milk (see also Soya drinks)

There are two concerns with milk. The first is whether the milk was produced using the milk-boosting hormone bovine somatotropin (BST) made with genetic engineering technology.

BST is not permitted to be used for UK or European Union dairy herds. There are concerns among EU veterinary advisers that the hormone causes animal welfare problems, and that use of the hormone may raise the levels of an autoimmune factor in the milk, which may then be linked to human health problems such as breast and prostate cancer.

The second issue is whether the animal was fed GM feed. Both maize and soya are common ingredients of animal feedstuffs, and it is quite likely that these will include GM soya and maize. The main exception to this is for food produced organically, as organic dairy herds should not be fed GM-produced material.

- ☑ all fresh organically produced milk
- ? Fresh and long-life milk (?feed)
- ? Fussell's Condensed Milk (?feed)
- ? Nestlé Condensed Milk (?feed)
- ☑ Skane UHT organic milk

Milk puddings (see also Custard)
There are several concerns about the use of GM processes in the production of milk and milk products; for more information, see Milk, above.

- ☑ Ambrosia Creamed Rice
- ☑ Ambrosia Creamed Tapioca/Semolina/Macaroni
- ? Birds Instant Semolina (modified starch, vegetable oils, cornflour)
- ? Farmlea Rice pudding (dextrose)
- ☑ Kallo rice pudding
- ? Müller Rice (modified starch)
- ☑ Plamil rice pudding
- ☑ Shape chilled creamy rice

Milkshakes and milk drinks (see also Hot beverages and Soya drinks and milk substitutes)
There are several concerns about the use of GM processes in the production of milk and milk products, including the use of a GM milk-boosting hormone called bovine somatotropin, and

questions about the contents of the animal feed used for the cattle. For more on this, see the section on Milk, above.

? Cadbury's Milk Chocolate Drink (vegetable oil, dried glucose syrup)

? Frijj (modified maize starch)

? Gulp (dextrose)

? Nesquick (glucose syrup)

✓ Yazoo

✓ Millet

Mineral water

Mineral waters should include no GM material, but some drinks describing themselves as flavoured mineral waters may include sweetening and colouring agents, which can be derived from maize, including GM maize.

✓ Silver Spring Flavoured Mineral Water

Miso (soyabean paste)

The main concern is that the soyabeans used may be GM. (See Soya, below.)

Mixers

These are flavoured soft drinks (see Soft drinks, below) which may include sweetening and colouring agents derived from maize starch, including GM maize.

? Canada Dry (caramel colouring)

✓ Schweppes Bitter Lemon, Tonic Water, Soda Water

? Schweppes Ginger Ale (caramel colouring)

Muesli

These are mixtures of grains and nuts, often with added sugar and with added milk powder (see Milk, above). Muesli does not usually include maize or soya products, but check the ingredients list on the labels.

✓ Alara organic

✓ Alpen

127

- ☑ Essential
- ☑ Familia organic
- ☑ Jordans organic
- ☑ Nature's Path organic
- ☑ Suma organic
- ☑ Traidcraft
- ☑ Tropical Wholefoods Magical Mango
- ☑ Whole Earth organic

Muffins

Like cakes generally, muffins are likely to be made with fats and oils that could be derived from GM sources, and may use lecithin emulsifier that could be derived from GM soyabeans.

- ☐ Speedibake muffins (vegetable oil, modified starch, xanthan gum, lecithin)
- ☐ Whitworth's Muffin Mix (vegetable oils, dextrose)

Mushrooms See Fungi

Mussels See Shellfish

Mustard

There are no GM mustard plants or seeds permitted to be sold in the UK. Most mustard is sold prepared as a blend of seeds and seed flour with vinegar and other ingredients such as herbs and sweetening agents. These sweetening agents may include sugars derived from maize starch, including GM-derived maize starch.

- ☑ Byodo
- ☑ Colmans English
- ☑ Gordons organic
- ☐ Maille (dextrose)

☑ Mustard and cress

Mutton See Meat

Naan See Bread

Nachos See Tortillas and Crisps

☑ **Nectarines**

Noodles
Noodles are normally prepared from plain wheat paste, although some may include egg, spinach or other ingredients. Noodles sold with sauces may include oils and other ingredients that could come from maize, soya or tomato paste, including GM versions. Frozen prepared noodles may include the sauce ready-mixed into the noodles.

☑ Amoy egg noodles
☑ Asian Home Gourmet Noodle Dinner
☐? Batchelors Super Noodles (vegetable oils)
☑ Blue Dragon
☐? Crosse & Blackwell frozen noodles (vegetable oil)
☑ The Noodle Company organic noodles
☐? Oriental Express frozen noodles (vegetable oil)
☒ Pot Noodles (vegetable oil, tomato paste, GM soya pieces, maltodextrin, soy sauce)
☑ Sharwoods noodles

☑ **Nuts** (see also Peanuts)
There are no GM nuts permitted to be sold in the UK. Salted or flavoured nuts may include vegetable oil, which may come from GM maize or soya, and flavour boosters such as hydrolysed vegetable protein or monosodium glutamate, which can be derived from soya, including GM soya.

☐? Blue Diamond Smoke House almonds (maltodextrin, hydrolysed vegetable protein)
☑ Cauldron nut cutlets
☑ Crazy Jack's organic nuts
☑ Equal Exchange chocolate Brazils
☑ Essential organic nuts
☑ Granose nut-roast mixes
☑ GranoVita nut luncheon
☑ Opie's pickled walnuts

☑ Percy Daltons peanuts in shell
☑ Percy Daltons organic salted cashew nuts, salted peanuts
☑ Rakusen's ground almonds
☑ Suma organic nuts, nut roast mix
☑ Traidcraft chocolate nut, raisins

Nut spreads (see also Chocolate spread and Peanut butter)
These normally include an added vegetable oil, which might be
from soya or maize, including GM soya or maize. They may also
be emulsified with lecithin or other emulsifiers that can be
derived from soya, including GM soya.
☑ Equal Exchange cashew butter
☑ Meridian nut butters
? Nutella (vegetable oils, lecithin)
☑ Stute Hazelnut and chocolate spread
☑ Whole Earth 3-Nut butter

Oatcakes (see also Biscuits and Crackers)
The oats will not be genetically modified as no GM oats are
permitted to be sold in the UK, but oatcakes also include oil, which
may be derived from maze or soya, including GM maize or soya.
? Nairn's (vegetable oil)
☑ Paterson Arran

☑ Oats
One of the world's main grain crops in cooler climates. There are
no GM oats permitted to be sold in the UK, but research is under
way to develop GM crossbreeds of wheat and oats to create
novel types of flour.
☑ Mornflake oats, oat bran.
☑ Quaker Oats
? Quaker Oatso Simple (lecithin)
☑ Scott's Porage Oats

Octopus See Squid

Offal See Meat

Oils See Fats and oils

☑ **Okra** (see also Tinned vegetables)

Olive oil See Fats and oils

☑ **Olives and olive paste**
No GM olives are permitted to be sold in the UK. Olives may come in a brine or oil-based liquid, and the oil may be from maize or soya, which might be from a GM source.
☑ all plain olives in brine
☑ Chalice olive appetisers and paste
☑ Cypressa plain and stuffed
☑ Sunita plain and stuffed, and olive pâté

☑ **Onions**
There are no GM onions permitted to be sold in the UK, but research is being undertaken on developing GM strains of onion resistant to the yellow dwarf virus.
☑ Garner's pickled onions
☑ Haywards pickled onions

Orangeade See Carbonated drinks and Soft drinks

☑ **Oranges**
There are no GM oranges permitted to be sold in the UK, but research is being undertaken on modifying the genes responsible for resisting citrus virus attack.

Orange squash See Soft drinks

☑☑ **Organic foods**
All organic foods are required to be free of GM ingredients and GM derivatives. Organic livestock must be reared without the use of animal feeds containing any GM material. Organic milk must be produced without the use of the GM-produced milk-boosting hormone bovine somatotropin (BST) and organic cheese must be

made without the use of GM chymosin or calves' rennet. For a list of suppliers of organic foods see our reading list.

Oysters See Shellfish

? Pancakes
Like breads and cakes, commercially made pancakes may include vegetable fats, soya flour, emulsifiers, and sweeteners such as glucose syrup, all of which might be derived from GM sources. Filled pancakes may include sauces made with cornflour, starches or sugars from maize, including GM maize, as well as vegetable oil, colourings and emulsifiers, all of which may be derived from GM sources.
? Sunblest sweet pancakes (vegetable fat)
? Findus and Crosse & Blackwell filled Crispy Pancakes (vegetable oil, tomato paste, modified starch, caramel colouring, dextrose)
✓ Whitworth's Pancake and Yorkshire Pudding Mix

✓ Papaya (pawpaw)
There is no GM papaya permitted to be sold in the UK, but a genetically modified papaya developed for resistance to viral attack is permitted to be grown in the USA and has been approved for food use.

✓ Parsley

✓ Parsnips

✓ Passion fruit

Pasta, canned and frozen
Although the pasta may be made purely from wheat, and hence will not be genetically modified, the sauce that accompanies the pasta may contain vegetable oil, thickening agents such as starch and cornflour, and tomato paste, all of which can be derived from GM sources.

? Action Man (tomato paste, modified cornflour, vegetable oil, maltodextrin, riboflavin)

? Dolmio frozen pasta dishes (tomato paste, modified maize starch)

? Findus frozen lasagne (tomato paste, modified starch, margarine, maltodextrin, vegetable oil)

? Heinz Macaroni Cheese (modified cornflour, vegetable oil)

? Heinz Spaghetti and Meatballs (cornflour)

? Postman Pat (tomato paste, modified starch, riboflavin)

? Teletubbies (tomato paste, modified cornflour, vegetable oil, maltodextrin, riboflavin)

? Thomas the Tank Engine (tomato paste, modified cornflour, vegetable oil, maltodextrin, riboflavin)

Pasta, dried and fresh

Plain pasta is made from durum wheat, and there are no varieties of GM wheat which are permitted to be sold in the UK. Pasta with added egg or spinach should also be free of GM ingredients, but pasta with tomato may have used a tomato paste from a GM source.

? Batchelors Pasta Soup and Pasta 'n' Sauce (tomato paste, vegetable oil, glucose syrup, cornflour)

✔ Buitoni

? Duetto (tomato paste, vegetable oil)

✔ Eunature organic

✔ Glutano gluten-free

✔ Helios

✔ La Bio-Idea organic

✔ La Terra organic

✔ Orgran gluten-free

? Signor Rossi (breadcrumbs, modified starch, vegetable oil)

✔ Stamp organic pasta

Pasties See Meat pies

Pastries See Doughnuts and pastries

Pastry (see also Doughnuts and pastries)
Pastry is a mix including flour and fat. The fat is usually vegetable fat, which may be derived from soya or maize, including GM soya or maize. The flour is usually wheat flour, but may be blended with soya and/or maize flours, including those from GM sources. Sweetened pastry usually uses sugar rather than sweeteners that may come from maize.

- [?] Green's Pastry Mix (vegetable oil)
- [✓] Homestead Foods spinach/mushroom pastry
- [?] Jus Rol pastry (vegetable oil)
- [✓] Jus Rol vol au vents
- [?] McDougall's Viota pastry mix (vegetable oil)

Pâtés and meat pastes
The main ingredients are derived from meat (see Meat, above) or vegetables with added thickening and sweetening agents, including some made from maize, possibly GM maize, and flavour boosters such as hydrolysed vegetable protein, which can be derived from soya or maize, including GM versions.

- [✓] Cauldron carrot/chickpea/spinach/tomato
- [✓] GranoVita vegetable spreads
- [?] Martier Duck Pâté (dextrose)
- [✓] Mattesson's Brussels Pâté
- [✗] Princes Beef/Chicken/Tuna Paste (GM soya protein, rusk, hydrolysed vegetable protein)
- [?] Shippams Beef/Chicken Spread (rusk)
- [✓] Suma vegetable pâtés
- [✓] Sunita olive pâté
- [✓] Tartex vegetable pâtés

Patties (see also Meat pies)
Patties are similar in composition to pies, with a pastry shell and sauce filling. The pastry is a mix including flour and fat, usually vegetable fat, which may be derived from soya or maize, including GM soya or maize. The flour is usually wheat flour, but may be blended with soya and/or maize flours, including those from GM sources.

? Island Brand Jamaican Pattie Delight Salt Fish/Chicken/Halal Lamb (rusk, vegetable fat)

☑ Caribbean Foods callaloo/vegetable patties

☑ Peaches

There are no GM peaches permitted to be sold in the UK, but research is being undertaken to isolate the genes responsible for peach ripening.

Peanut butter (see also Nut spreads)

The peanuts in peanut butter should not be genetically modified as no GM varieties of peanuts are permitted to be sold in the UK. Some manufacturers add vegetable oils, usually palm fat but occasionally from sources such as soya or maize, including GM soya or maize. Some manufacturers use emulsifying agents that may also be derived from soya, including GM soya.

☑ Equal Exchange

☑ Essential organic

☑ Meridian

☑ Suma

? Sun Pat (emulsifiers)

☑ Traidcraft

☑ Whole Earth

Peanuts

There are no GM peanuts permitted to be sold in the UK, but research is being undertaken on inserting a toxin into peanuts that slows the growth of insects that attempt to eat the peanut, preventing the insect larvae developing into adults. Many roasted peanuts come with a coating of vegetable oil, which may be maize or soya oil, including GM maize or soya oil, and some peanuts – such as dry-roasted nuts – may have added flavour boosters such as monosodium glutamate, which can be derived from soya, including GM soya.

☑ Essential organic peanuts

? KP Peanuts (vegetable oil)

? KP Nutsters (starch, vegetable oil, modified starch,

monosodium glutamate)
[?] KP Dry Roasted nuts (monosodium glutamate, modified
starch, dextrose)
[✔] Percy Daltons peanuts in shell
[✔] Percy Daltons organic salted peanuts

[✔] **Pears** (see also Tinned fruit)
There are no GM pears permitted to be sold in the UK, but
research is being undertaken on a GM apple-pear cross with
resistance to fungal disease.

[✔] **Peas** (see also Frozen vegetables and Tinned vegetables)
There are no GM peas permitted to be sold in the UK, but field
trials are being undertaken in the USA.

Peppercorns See Herbs and spices

[✔] **Peppers (bell peppers, capsicums) and chillies
(chilli peppers)**
There are no GM peppers of any variety permitted to be sold in
the UK, but research is under way on modifying the pepper
genes to enhance disease resistance. Some preserved peppers
are bottled in oils, which may include vegetable oil from maize or
soya, including GM maize or soya.

Pet food
Most manufacturers of pet food change the sources of their
ingredients according to what is available at low cost at any
given time, and this may vary from week to week. Both the
vegetable and animal ingredients in pet food may be of concern:
the vegetable origins may easily be from soya or maize crops, as
is a substantial amount of farm-animal feed, and in this case the
crops could include GM versions. The animal derivatives found in
pet food are likely to come from animals that themselves have
been fed on maize or soya feed, including GM maize and soya.
As we suggest in Meat, above, modified gene fragments can
cross from the gut to the organs of the animal, so in theory all

animals fed with GM crops may carry some modified gene material, if only for a short time. Animals reared organically are not permitted to be fed with GM material.

CAT FOOD
☐ Pedigree (Whiskas, Brekkies, Katkins, Kitekat, Sheba)
☐ Ralston Purina (Kit N Kaboodle, Cat Chow)
☐ Spillers (Felix, Arthurs, Friskies, Go Cat, Choosy, Gourmet Gold)

DOG FOOD
☐ Heinz Snausages
☑ Happidog Health Food
☑ Pampered Pets vegetarian dog food
☐ Pedigree (Chappies, Chum, Bounce, Pal, Cesar)
☐ Ralston Purina (Bakers Power Crunch/Light/Complete, Dog Chow)
☐ Spillers (Friskies, Chunky, Butch, Winalot)
☑ Wafcol
☑ Yarrah vegetarian organic dog food

Pheasant and partridge See Game

Piccallili
Watch out for thickening agents, such as starch, and sweetening agents, such as glucose syrup, both of which may be derived from GM maize. Foods coloured yellow may use GM riboflavin colouring (E101).
☐ Haywards Piccallili (modified starch)

Pickles
☑ Baxters pickled beetroot
☐ Branston Pickle (tomato paste, modified starch)
☐ Branston Sandwich Pickle (modified starch, caramel colouring)
☑ Delicias Banderilas pickles on sticks
☑ Garner's pickled onions

☑ Haywards pickled onions, gherkins
☑ Opie's pickled walnuts
☑ Parson's pickled cockles, mussels

Pies, fruit See Fruit pies

Pies, meat See Meat pies

Pigeon See Game

☑ **Pilchards** (see also Tinned fish)

☑ **Pineapple** (see also Tinned fruit)
There are no GM pineapples permitted for sale in the UK, but research on GM pineapples is being undertaken to improve yields.

Pistachio See Nuts

Pitta bread See Bread

Pizzas
The base for a pizza is similar in content to bread (see Bread, above) in which case the vegetable oils and sweetening agents may come from maize or soya, including GM maize or soya, and there are continuing questions over the use of GM yeast – approved by UK government advisers in 1990 but understood not to be in commercial production. Pizza toppings usually include cheese (see Cheese, above) and tomato paste (see Tomatoes, below) and may be thickened with starches derived from maize, including GM maize.
❓ Chicago Town Pepperoni Deep Frozen Pizza (cheese, maize flour, vegetable oil, modified starch, dextrose)
❓ Findus French Bread Pizza (vegetable oil, invert sugar syrup, dextrose, tomato paste, modified starch, vegetable oil)
❓ Goodfella's (cheese, tomato paste, vegetable oils, modified starch)

? McCaines Deep Frozen Pizza (tomato paste, breadcrumbs, vegetable oil, modified starch)
? Napolina Pizza Base (margarine, dextrose)
? New York Pizza Bagels (tomato paste, vegetable oil, modified starch, xanthan gum)
? San Marco Pizza Slices (modified starch, cheese, tomato paste)
✔ Whole Earth pizza base

Plaice See Fish

✔ Plantains

✔ Plums
There are no GM plums permitted for sale in the UK, but research is being conducted on GM plums, and on a GM combination of apricot and plum.

Polenta See Maize

✔ Pomegranates

Popcorn
The corn (maize) variety used for popping corn is understood not to be the GM maize permitted in the UK, so there should be no GM popcorn permitted in the UK. Ready-to-eat popcorn is usually prepared in vegetable oil, which may include soya or maize oil, and these might be from GM crops. Sweetened popcorn may include glucose syrup or other sugars that can be derived from maize, including from GM maize.

? Butterkist (glucose syrup, vegetable fat, lecithin)
? ConAgra Microwave Popcorn (vegetable oil)
✔ Cypressa popping corn
✔ Dunn's River popping corn
? Ginni's Toffee Popcorn (glucose syrup, vegetable oil, lecithin)
✔ Sea Island popping corn

Poppadums

These are crisp-fried flour products. The flour is usually from rice, dhal (lentils) or potato, and therefore should be free of any GM material as no GM rice, potato or dhal is permitted to be sold in the UK. The oil or fat in which poppadums are fried may, however, be derived from maize or soya, which may include GM maize or soya.

☑ Natco
☑ Sharwoods plain

Pork See Meat

Pork pies See Meat pies

☑ **Potatoes** (see also Chips and Crisps and bag snacks)

There are no GM varieties of potato permitted for sale in the UK. GM potato crops are now being grown commercially in other parts of the world, and this may lead to new sources of GM material entering the UK food supply, such as starches and modified starches made from GM potatoes which will be virtually impossible to distinguish from starches obtained from non-GM potatoes. GM insect-resistant potatoes are approved for growing in Japan and the USA, and another version is approved for growing in Canada. Potatoes with altered starch structure are being developed – they promise reduced fat absorption, allowing consumers to enjoy chips and crisps with, it is claimed, a lower fat content.

☑ all plain potatoes
☑ Greenacres potato products
❓ Mr Mash (emulsifiers, riboflavin)
❓ Smash (emulsifiers)

Prawns See Shellfish

Preserves See Jams and conserves and Pickles

Prunes See Dried fruit

Puddings See Desserts and Tinned puddings

Pulses See Beans and Lentils and dhal

☑ **Pumpkins and squashes**
There are no GM pumpkins or squashes permitted for sale in the UK, but two types of GM squash have been approved for growing commercially in the USA, both of them developed to be resistant to viral attack.

☑ **Pumpkin seeds**

Quail See Game

Quiche (see also Pastry, Milk, Eggs and Cheese)
The pastry may contain unspecified vegetable oils and soya flour, which may come from GM sources. The filling may be thickened with starches and may use emulsifiers, both of which may be derived from GM sources.
❓ Freshbake (vegetable oil, modified starch)

☑ **Quince** (see also Jams and conserves)

☑ **Quinoa**

Quorn
Quorn is a food invented this century, and created from a type of fungus grown with a solution of glucose syrup. The glucose syrup could be derived from maize starch, including starch from GM maize.
❓ Quorn fillets, sausages and burgers (?glucose syrup process, rusk, vegetable oil, starch or modified starch)
❓ Quorn mince and pieces (?glucose syrup process)

Rabbit See Game and Meat

☑ **Radishes and mooli**

Raisin loaf See Bread or Malt loaf

Raisins See Dried fruit

☑ **Raspberries** (see also Tinned fruit)
There are no GM raspberries permitted for sale in the UK, but research is being undertaken into creating GM raspberries resistant to virus attack, and GM raspberries with slower ripening and decaying properties, allowing longer shelf lives and easier transportation.

Ready meals
Many ready meals rely on ingredients such as gums and starches to thicken sauces and prevent them separating, and flavour boosters to enhance the flavour of processed, long-shelf-life ingredients. The vegetable oils, starches and gums, sweetening agents, colouring agents, emulsifiers and flavour enhancers may be derived from maize or starch, including GM maize and starch. Most supermarkets are now phasing out the use of GM ingredients in their own-brand ready meals.
? Batchelors Pasta 'n' Sauce (tomato powder, vegetable oil)
? Findus Lean Cuisine ready meals (vegetable oil, soya sauce, modified starch, fructose syrup, margarine, caramel colouring)
? Heinz Weight Watchers ready meals (vegetable oil, modified cornflour, maltodextrin)
? Linda McCartney dishes (vegetable oil, hydrolysed vegetable protein)
? Quorn Lasagne, Chilli (?glucose syrup process, rusk, vegetable oil, starch, tomato purée)
? Tyne Brand Irish Stew (soya protein isolate)
✗ Vesta Beef Curry and Chow Mein (GM soya mince, maize starch, modified starch)
? Vesta Beef Risotto and Chicken Supreme (maize starch, modified starch)
? Westlers Tinned Curry Meals (tomato paste, soya lecithin, vegetable oil, modified starch, dextrose, modified maize starch)

☑ **Redcurrants**

Relishes See Sauces

☑ **Rhubarb** (see also Tinned fruit)

☑ **Rice**
There is no GM rice permitted for sale in the UK, but research is under way on the use of genes from grasses and other plants to develop varieties of rice that do not need to reproduce through pollination (apomixis), and a GM variety of rice that crosses Basmati and a semi-dwarf strain has been patented by a Texas company. GM rice crops grown commercially elsewhere in the world may lead to new sources of GM material entering the UK food supply, such as starches and modified starches made from GM rice, and these will be difficult to distinguish from starches obtained from non-GM sources. Research is already under way to develop GM crossbreeds of wheat and rice to create novel types of flour. Rice products prepared with extra ingredients may include vegetable oil, sauce thickeners and colouring, and flavour-boosting ingredients that can be derived from maize and soya, including GM maize and soya.

☑ Asian Home Gourmet Rice Dinner
❓ Batchelors Rices of the World, Original Rice (soy sauce powder, vegetable oil, tomato paste, maltodextrin)
☑ Country Harvest organic rice
☑ Tilda
☑ Uncle Bens regular
❓ Uncle Bens Express for Microwave (vegetable oil)
☑ Ye Olde Oak Ready Rice dishes

Rice pudding See Milk puddings

Roe (see also Caviar and Taramasalata)
Roe are the eggs of fish such as cod and herring. No GM varieties of fish or their roe are permitted in the UK. Processed roe may be prepared in oil and sauces that can contain

ingredients derived from soya, maize or tomato, including GM
varieties.
[?] John West Compressed Cod Roe (vegetable oil)

Rolls See Bread

[✓] **Runner beans**

Rusks
Rusks are based on bread, although they may not always contain
the full complement of bread ingredients (see Bread, above).
Rusk is a common ingredient as a bulking agent in processed
meats, such as sausages.
[?] Farley's Baby Rusks (vegetable oil, riboflavin)

[✓] **Rye**
One of the world's main grain crops. There is no GM rye permitted
for sale in the UK, but research is under way to develop GM
crossbreeds of wheat and rye to create novel types of flour.

[✓] **Sago** (see also Milk puddings)
Sago are small balls of starch prepared from the inner trunk of
various types of palm tree.
[✓] Whitworth's sago

Salad creams (see also Mayonnaise)
These are a blend of oil with vinegar, flavouring and other
ingredients, including thickening agents. The oil and the
thickening agents may be derived from maize or soya, including
GM maize or soya.
[✓] Alavon
[?] Heinz (vegetable oil, modified cornflour, riboflavin)
[✓] Plamil egg-free
[?] Waistline (modified starch, riboflavin)

Salad dressings
These are a blend of oils, vinegar and flavouring ingredients, and

some versions may include tomato. The vegetable oil may be derived from maize or starch, including GM maize or starch, and the tomato paste may be derived from GM tomatoes.

- ☑ Bionova
- ? Kraft Thousand Island (vegetable oil, tomato paste)
- ☑ Kraft Vinaigrette
- ☑ Meridian Organic French Dressing
- ☑ Tropic Isle dressings
- ☑ Whole Earth American organic

Salads

There are no GM salad vegetables permitted to be sold in the UK, but research is under way into creating GM salad vegetables with greater resistance to pests, greater tolerance of pesticide sprays, and slower decaying properties giving them a longer shelf life and greater transportation potential. Ready-to-eat salads may consist of the vegetables you expect, but some may be ready dressed, and the dressing could include oils, thickeners and sweeteners derived from maize or soya, including GM maize or soya.

- ? Delphi Couscous Salad (vegetable oil)
- ☑ Florette leaf salads

Salami

These are mixtures of meat (see Meat, above) with flavourings, spices and sweeteners. Some include sugars such as dextrose which can be derived from maize, including GM maize. The flavourings may include monosodium glutamate, which can be derived from soya, including GM soya.

- ? Bistro (monosodium glutamate)
- ? Cittero (dextrose)
- ? Peperami (glucose, monosodium glutamate)
- ☑ Revilla chorizo

? Salmon (see also Smoked fish)

No GM salmon is permitted to be sold in the UK, but research is being undertaken on altering the growth rate of farmed fish using gene technology, creating much faster-growing and larger fish. One concern at present is the feed being given to farm-reared salmon, which may include meat derivatives from animals that are in turn fed maize or soya, including GM maize or soya.

☑ Salsify

Salt

Salt is a mineral with no genetic structure, so cannot be genetically modified. Salt is used widely to enhance the flavour of processed foods, which may themselves include GM-derived ingredients.

Sandwiches (see also Bread, Fats and oils, Sandwich fillers and specific filling ingredients)

Commercially produced, wrapped sandwiches must be labelled with details of their contents, including any detectable GM ingredients made with maize or soya.

Sandwich fillers

Pastes and spreads designed to be used in sandwiches may be made with vegetable oils and thickeners derived from maize and soya, including GM maize and soya. The meat content might be linked to GM sources if the animals from which it is derived were themselves fed with GM material.

- ? Branston Sandwich Pickle (modified starch, caramel colouring)
- ? Heinz Sandwich Fillers (vegetable oil, modified cornflour)
- ? Heinz Sandwich Spread (vegetable oil, modified cornflour)
- ? Shippams Sandwich Fillers (vegetable oil, starch)
- ? Shippams Beef/Chicken Spread (rusk)
- ✗ Princes Beef/Chicken/Tune Paste (GM soya protein, rusk, hydrolysed vegetable protein)
- ? Smedley's Sandwich Filling (vegetable oil, xanthan gum)

☑ Sardines (see also Tinned fish)

Fresh sardines should be GM free as no GM pilchards are permitted to be sold in the UK.

Sauces (see also Gravy)
Both cooking sauces and table sauces are likely to include
starches and vegetable fats derived from soya or maize, which
might include GM soya or maize. They may also include tomato
paste, gums, colourings and emulsifiers which could have been
derived from GM crops.

COOKING SAUCES

[?] Amoy Stir-Fry sauces (modified starch, soyabean oil, soy
sauce, hydrolysed vegetable protein, soyabeans, caramel
colouring, tomato paste)

[?] Birds Brandy Flavour Sauce Mix (modified starch, vegetable
oil)

[✔] Bisto Chip Shop Curry Sauce

[?] Bisto Sauce Granules (vegetable oil, lecithin)

[?] Campbell's Texas Salsa Sauce (tomato paste)

[?] Chicken Tonight (modified starch, tomato paste, fructose,
glucose, caramel colouring, riboflavin)

[?] Colemans Cook-in Sauces and Casserole mixes (modified
starch, cornflour, tomato paste, vegetable oil)

[?] Dolmio Pasta Sauce and Stir-In Sauce (tomato paste,
modified starch, vegetable oil)

[?] Emperor's Palace frozen sauces (modified starch, tomato
paste, soy sauce, vegetable oil)

[✔] Frens Curry pastes

[✔] Gia Green Pesto

[✔] Go Organic

[?] Homepride Cook-in Sauces (modified starch, tomato purée,
vegetable oil)

[✘] Homepride Potato Bake Cook-in Sauce (cornstarch, GM soya
protein)

[✔] Kitchen Garden organic

[?] Knorr Pasta Sauce (tomato paste, vegetable oil, modified starch)

[✔] Lee Kum Kee vegetarian sauces

[✔] Loyd Grossman sauces

[?] Madhur Jaffrey (Tilda) (vegetable oil, tomato paste)

[✔] McCormick pasta sauces

☑ Meridian Organic Pasta Sauce
☑ Meridian Salsa, Balti and Rogan sauces
☑ Mr Bean
☑ Muir Glen
❓ Napolina Spicy Pizza Topping (tomato paste, modified starch, vegetable oil)
❓ Old El Paso Taco Salsa (tomato paste, modified starch)
❓ Old El Paso Burrito Cook-in Sauce (tomato paste, dextrose, rusk, modified starch)
☑ Pastaking pasta sauces
☑ Pataks Curry paste
❓ Ragu Pasta Sauce (tomato paste, dextrose)
❓ Schwarz Cook-in Sauces (vegetable fat, modified starch, maltodextrin, hydrolysed vegetable protein, soya protein)
☒ Sharwoods Black Bean Stir-in Sauce includes GM soya
❓ Sharwoods Curry Sauces (vegetable oil, tomato paste, modified corn starch, soya flour)
❓ Sharwoods Stir-Fry Sauces (modified cornstarch, vegetable oil, tomato paste, soy sauce, soyabeans)
❓ Uncle Bens Korma Sauce (tomato paste, vegetable oil, modified starch, vegetable fat, lecithin)
❓ Uncle Bens Stir Fry Sauce (vegetable oil, modified starch, soy sauce, caramel colouring, lecithin)
❓ Valfrutta Salsina (tomato paste)
☑ Vegetarian World pasta sauces
☑ Whole Earth
❓ Wing Yip Chinese sauces (modified starch, corn starch, soya protein, vegetable oil)
☑ Zest

RELISHES AND TABLE SAUCES

These, too, may contain ingredients from maize or soya, which might include GM maize or soya. Typical formulations are: horseradish sauce (vegetable oil, xanthan gum), mint sauce (xanthan gum, riboflavin), tartare sauce (vegetable oil, modified starch) and seafood sauce (tomato paste, vegetable oil).
❓ Amoy Soy Sauce (soya)

SAUCES – SEA VEGETABLES AND SEAWEED

- ？ Chef's tomato ketchup (modified starch)
- ？ Colmans Tartare Sauce (vegetable oil, modified starch)
- ？ Colmans Bramley Apple Sauce (modified starch)
- ？ Daddies Brown Sauce (modified starch)
- ？ Encona Hot Pepper Sauce Original (corn starch)
- ✔ Encona Hot Pepper Sauce Smooth, Cajun and Banana
- ✔ Grace Hot Pepper sauce
- ？ Heinz tomato ketchup (glucose syrup)
- ？ HP Sauce (tomato paste, cornflour, soy sauce)
- ？ Jamaica Best (xanthan gum)
- ✔ Kitchen Garden
- ✔ Lea & Perrins Worcestershire Sauce
- ✔ McIlhenny's Tabasco
- ✔ Meridian Organic Ketchup
- ？ Ocean Spray Cranberry Sauce (glucose syrup)
- ？ Sharwoods Hot Chilli Sauce (modified corn starch)
- ✔ Whole Earth

？ Sausage rolls

A combination of pastry and sausage meat (see Pastry, above, and Meat products, above) sausage rolls are likely to include vegetable fat, and may include soya flour and soya protein, all of which could be derived from GM soya.

Sausages See Meat products and Vegetarian products

Savoury snacks See Crisps and bag snacks

Scallops See Shellfish

Scampi See Shellfish

Seasoning See Herbs and spices

Sea vegetables and seaweed
- ✔ Clearspring
- ✔ Muso

☑ Sea Greens Co
☑ Western Isle

Semolina (see also Milk puddings)

Semolina is coarsely milled wheat, and no GM wheat is permitted to be sold in the UK.

☑ Whitworth's Semolina

Sesame (see also Fats and oils)

Sesame seeds and products such as tahini (sesame paste) usually come without additional ingredients, but sesame seeds are sometimes made into sweet bars (using sweeteners including glucose syrup, which may be derived from GM maize) and sesame paste may be made into a sweet confection called halva.

? Agros Sesame Snaps (glucose syrup)
☑ Bombay halva
☑ Cypressa tahini, halva
☑ Equal Exchange Barrita sesame bar
? Elite Halva (glucose syrup, soya protein)
☑ Equal Exchange tahini
☑ Essential organic tahini
☑ Meridian tahini
☑ Suma tahini
☑ Sunita halva, tahini

Shellfish

There are no GM shellfish permitted to be sold in the UK, but the sauces and coatings used on shellfish may contain vegetable oil and starch and other ingredients that might come from genetically modified crops. The term 'crabsticks' and 'surimi' refer to reconstituted fish flakes with added flavouring (which may include monosodium glutamate, which can be derived from GM soya).

? Bantry Bay mussels in garlic butter (starch)
☑ Carrokeel mussels in garlic butter
☑ John West Crabmeat
? Kintyre breaded lobster (starch, maize flour, vegetable oil,

soya flour)

☑ Lyons Hot and Spicy Prawns (vegetable oil, maize flour, starch)

☑ Lyons King Prawn Rolls (vegetable oil)

✔ Marina mussels

✔ Oriental & Pacific tinned clams

✔ Parson's pickled Cockles and Mussels

✔ Peeled prawns

☑ Seafood Company breaded king prawns (dextrose, soya oil, cornflour, tomato paste)

✔ Spinnaker Mussels in Garlic

☒ Young's Pacific Island Lobster Wholetails (vegetable oil, rusk, modified starch, GM soya flour)

Skate See Fish

Slimming and diet foods

Generally these are similar to their non-slimming counterparts, but with some or all of the fats and oils replaced by other thickening ingredients such as gums and starches, which may be derived from maize, including GM maize. Some of the sugar may be replaced with artificial sweeteners. Some slimming foods are also fortified with extra vitamins and minerals, including the vitamin B2, riboflavin, which may have been produced using GM processes.

☑ Batchelors Slim-a-Soup (tomato paste, glucose syrup, cornflour, vegetable oil)

☑ Boots Shapers snack foods: Crispy Caramel Bar, Crisps (lecithin, polydextrose, vegetable oil)

☑ Findus Lean Cuisine ready meals (vegetable oil, soy sauce, modified starch, fructose syrup, margarine, caramel colouring)

☑ Heinz Weight Watchers frozen cheesecake (vegetable oil, glucose syrup, modified cornfllour, margarine, lecithin)

☑ Heinz Weight Watchers ready meals (vegetable oil, modified cornflour, maltodextrin)

☑ Slimfast (corn oil, riboflavin)

☑ Waistline Salad Cream (modified starch, riboflavin)

151

Smoked fish

No GM fish are permitted to be sold in the UK. Some smoked fish is coloured, and may be prepared in a sauce – in which case the oil and sauce thickening agents may be derived from maize or soya, including GM maize or soya.

☑ Macrae's smoked haddock and kipper fillets

Smoked meat See Bacon, Ham, Meat and Salami

Snack foods (see also Peanuts and Crisps and bag snacks)
This is a category of assorted products designed for immediate consumption with or without added hot water. They are likely to include starches and oils from undefined sources, and these sources may include GM crops.

❓ Batchelors Cup-a-Soup (tomato paste, glucose syrup, cornflour, vegetable oil)

❓ Knorr Taste Breaks (vegetable oil, maltodextrin, tomato paste)

❓ Kraft Dairylea Dunkers (corn vegetable oil)

❓ Kraft Philadelphia Handysnacks (breadsticks, vegetable oil)

❓ Kraft Snack Lunchables (vegetable oil, glucose syrup)

✗ Pot Noodles (vegetable oil, tomato paste, GM soya pieces, maltodextrin, soy sauce)

❓ Shape cottage cheese with Ryvita (maize starch in fruit version, and kibbled soya in Ryvita multigrain version)

❓ Snack Pasta (tomato powder, vegetable oil, glucose syrup)

❓ Snack Soup (vegetable oil, modified starch, maltodextrin, tomato paste)

☑ Snails

There are no GM snails on sale in the UK, but snails may be sold in sauces that could include vegetable oil or starches, which may be derived from GM crops.

Soft drinks (see also Carbonated drinks and Fruit juices)
As with carbonated drinks, juice drinks and ice lollies, these products are a mixture of sweetening agent with water, flavouring

and colouring agents. The sweetening agents may include sugars such as glucose or fructose that can be derived from maize starch, including GM-derived maize starch.

- ☑ C-Vit
- ☑ Gusto
- ❓ Kia Ora (fructose, glucose syrup)
- ❓ Ribena (carton) (glucose syrup)
- ☑ Ribena Tooth Kind
- ❓ Robinsons Fruit Squashes, Barley Drinks (fructose, glucose)
- ☑ Roses Lime Cordial
- ❓ Schweppes Cordials (glucose syrup)
- ❓ Vimto Cordial (glucose, fructose)

Sole See Fish

☑ Sorghum

One of the world's main grain crops, most of which is fed to animals. There is no GM sorghum permitted for sale in the UK, but research is under way on the use of genes from grasses and other plants to develop varieties of sorghum that do not need to reproduce through pollination, and research on drought-, insect- and disease-resistant strains is currently in progress.

Soups, canned or chilled

Tinned and chilled soups are usually thickened with starches or gums, which might be derived from GM maize. Some varieties might include tomato, which may be derived from GM tomato paste.

- ❓ Baxters (modified flour, cornflour, tomato paste)
- ❓ Campbell's (modified starch, vegetable oil, tomato purée)
- ☑ Go Organic organic soups
- ❓ Heinz (modified cornflour)
- ☑ Mr Bean
- ☑ New Covent Garden
- ☑ Pataks
- ☑ Suma organic soups

Soups, instant or dried

Packet soups are usually based on a mixture of starch, fat and salt, with some dried vegetable or meat powders and flavour boosters. The starches and fats may have been derived from maize or soya, including GM maize or soya. Some varieties may include tomato powder, which could be derived from GM tomato paste.

? Batchelors Soup, Cup-a-Soup, Slim-a-Soup, Cup-a-Soup Extra and Pasta Soup (tomato paste, glucose syrup, cornflour, vegetable oil)

☑ Just Wholefoods instant organic soups

? Knorr (soy sauce, tomato paste, modified starch, riboflavin)

Soya

The first mass-market GM crop, the Round-Up Ready soyabean, now covers 50% of the soya-growing plains of the USA and is also grown on a large scale in Argentina. Soyabean derivatives include soya oil, soya protein (including textured vegetable protein and hydrolysed vegetable protein), emulsifiers such as lecithin, and flavour boosters such as monosodium glutamate, plus soy sauce, tamari. tofu, tempeh and soyabean milk.

Further genetic modification of soya is being researched. New varieties resistant to other herbicides, virus and insect attack and tolerant of sub-freezing temperatures, are being tested in the USA. Other modified varieties have altered protein and oil profiles for nutritional improvement.

☑ organically produced soyabeans

Soya drinks and milk substitutes

These are made from soya oil and other extracts, and may be blended with other ingredients to add texture and flavour to the drink. The main concern is whether the soyabeans are from GM sources.

☑ Allergy Care soya shakes

☑ Granose soya drinks

☑ GranoVita soya drinks

☑ Imagine rice drinks

- ☑ Mill Milk oat drinks
- ☑ Plamil soya drinks
- ☑ Pro-Soya So Nice soya drinks
- ☑ Provamel soya drinks
- ☑ Rice Dream
- ❓ So Good soya drinks (maltodextrin, fructose, emulsifiers, riboflavin)
- ☑ Soya Health Foods soya drinks
- ☑ Sunrise soya milk
- ☑ Unisoy soya drink

Soya oil See Fats and oils

Soy sauce, shoyu and tamari (see also Sauces)
These are a salty fermentation from soyabeans or from hydrolysed vegetable protein (probably soya-derived). The source of soya may include GM crops. Some commercial varieties may also include caramel colouring, which may be derived from maize, including GM maize.
- ❓ Amoy Soy Sauce (soya)
- ☑ Clearspring shoyu, tamari
- ☑ Essential organic shoyu, tamari
- ❓ Kikkoman Soy Sauce (soya)
- ☑ Muso organic
- ❓ Superior Soy Sauce (soya, monosodium glutamate)

Spaghetti See Pasta

Spices See Herbs and spices

☑ **Spinach** (see also Tinned vegetables)
There is no GM spinach permitted to be sold in the UK, but research on GM spinach resistant to sub-freezing temperatures is under way.

Spirits and liqueurs See Alcoholic Drinks

Sports foods and drinks, energy and fortified drinks

There are several types of beverage that are sold for specialist purposes, including ones that imply that they can boost energy or sports prowess or provide supplemental nutrients. Generally these have a similar profile to soft drinks in terms of the likelihood of containing GM ingredients – i.e. the sweeteners and colouring agents can be derived from starches such as maize starch, which might include GM-derived maize starch.

? Lipovitan B3 (riboflavin)

? Lucozade Sport (dextrose, maltodextrin, glucose syrup)

? Mighty Malt (glucose syrup, riboflavin, caramel colouring)

? Nurishment (vegetable oil, riboflavin)

? Nutrament (vegetable oil, glucose syrup, soya protein, lecithin, riboflavin)

✓ Purdey's High Energy Gold

? Red Bull (glucose, caramel colouring)

? Red Devil (fructose, riboflavin)

? Supermalt (glucose syrup, riboflavin, caramel colouring)

? Vita Malt (caramel colouring)

Sprats See Fish

✓ Spring greens

There are no GM spring greens permitted to be sold in the UK, but the development of GM sprouts, cabbage and spring greens resistant to pests is being undertaken.

Spring rolls See Chinese-style food

Squash See Pumpkins and squashes

Squashes (fruit) See Soft drinks

Squid

Octopus and squid are not bred in captivity and have not been the subject of commercial genetic modification. Products made from these creatures may include sauces and coatings that

contain starches, flours, vegetable fats, etc, which could be from
GM sources (see also Fish and Fish products).

[?] Lyon's battered calamari (cornflour)

Starch See Thickeners

Steak See Beef, Beefburgers, Meat, Meat pies and Tinned meat

Stock cubes See Gravy and Sauces

☑ **Strawberries**
There are no GM strawberries permitted to be sold in the UK, but
field trials of GM strawberries are being conducted in the USA.
Researchers are currently looking at ways of genetically
modifying strawberries to increase their sweetness.

Stuffing mixes
These are a mixture of flour and fat with added flavouring
ingredients. The flour may include starches from maize, including
GM maize, and the fat may include oils from maize or soya,
including GM maize or soya. The flavourings may include flavour
enhancers such as hydrolysed vegetable protein, which can be
derived from soya or maize, including GM soya or maize.

☑ Just Wholefoods stuffing mixes
[?] Paxo (rusk, vegetable suet, vegetable oil, hydrolysed
vegetable protein)
[?] Whitworth's Cook in the Pan stuffing (vegetable oil,
maltodextrin, hydrolysed vegetable protein)
[?] Whitworth's Stuffits (vegetable oil)

Suet See Fats and oils

☑ **Sugar**
Sugar can be derived from sugar beet or sugar cane. At present
neither source of sugar is genetically modified. British Sugar (the
company that provides the seed for the entire UK sugar beet
crop) says it has no plans to use GM varieties for commercial

sugar production, although there are experimental tests of herbicide-resistant varieties of sugar beet under way. Field trials of GM sugar cane are also under way, though these are not approved for food use.

Sugar substitutes
Artificial sweeteners are very intense and only a small quantity is needed to sweeten a drink. In order to bulk out the product, some manufacturers use starches, which may be derived from maize, including GM maize.

- [?] Canderel (maltodextrin)
- [?] Gold Sweet (maltodextrin)
- [✓] Hermisetas

Sultanas See Dried fruit

Sunflower oil See Fats and oils

[✓] Sunflower seeds
There are no GM sunflowers or sunflower seeds permitted to be sold in the UK, but field trials of GM sunflower varieties are under way in the USA.

Sunflower spreads See Fats and oils

Supplements See Vitamins and supplements

[✓] Swedes

Sweet and sour sauce See Sauces

[✓] Sweetcorn (see also Tinned vegetables and Frozen vegetables)
The varieties of maize that produce sweetcorn do not include the genetically modified variety permitted for use in the UK food supply, and no GM sweetcorn is permitted for sale in the UK. Trials of GM sweetcorn are being held on UK farms, and there

has been some concern among farmers – especially organic farmers – that pollen from the GM trial crops could be spreading to their own crops.

☑ fresh sweetcorn
☑ Green Giant tinned sweetcorn

Sweeteners See Sugar substitutes

☑ Sweet potatoes

There are no GM sweet potatoes permitted for sale in the UK, but field trials of GM sweet potatoes are under way in the USA.

Sweets See Chocolate and confectionery

Syrups

Most syrup sold to shoppers is based on cane sugar, which will be GM free. Syrups used in food processing, however, may be derived from maize starch, including GM-derived maize starch.

☑ Clearspring barley, rice and cornsyrup
☑ Essential Trading molasses and malt extract
☑ Meridian date and maple syrups and molasses
☑ Tate & Lyle
☑ Whole Earth barley, maize and rice syrup

Tacos

These are maize-based crisp biscuits, containing maize and vegetable oil. The maize may be from GM sources, and the oil may be from soya or maize, including GM soya or maize. The sauces accompanying some tacos may include more vegetable oil and tomato paste, which could be GM-derived tomato paste.

? Old El Paso Taco Dinner (corn, tomato paste)
? Old El Paso Tacos (cornflour, vegetable oil)
? Old El Paso Taco Salsa (tomato paste, modified starch)

Tahini See Sesame

☑ Tangerines

☑ Tapioca

Tapioca is the extracted starch from the roots of a leafy shrub found originally in Latin America. There are no GM varieties of tapioca – neither the tapioca granules nor the original plants – permitted to be sold in the UK.

Taramasalata (see also Caviar and Roe)
This is a paste including fish roe and oil, which may be an oil from maize or soya, including GM maize or soya.
☐ Delphi Taramosalata (vegetable oil, rusk)
☐ Lava/Zorba Taramosalata (vegetable oil, breadcrumbs)

☑ Taro (dasheen)

☑ Tea (see also Herbal and fruit teas)

There are no GM varieties of tea permitted to be sold in the UK. Products such as instant teas may have added ingredients that are derived from maize or soya, including GM maize or soya.
☑ Brooke Bond
☑ Clipper Organic
☐ Lift Instant Lemon Tea (dextrose)
☑ PG Tips
☑ PG Tips Instant Tea
☑ Ridgeways Organic
☑ Tetley Tea Granules
☑ Twinings
☑ Twinings Iced Peach Tea
☑ Typhoo
☐ Typhoo QT Instant Tea (dried glucose syrup, vegetable oil)

Tempeh

Tempeh is made from fermented soyabeans. The main concern is the source of the beans, as these may be from GM crops.
☑ Yakso organic

Textured vegetable protein (see also Vegetarian products)

This material is usually made from defatted soya flour but might also be derived from maize flour, and in both cases the main concern is the source of the soya or maize, as this may be from GM crops. TVP is commonly used in meat substitutes and vegetarian foods, and to extend meat products.

☑ Essential Trading TVP mince, chunks – plain, flavoured and organic.

☑ Suma TVP mince, chunks – plain and meat flavour.

Thickeners and gels (see also Sauces)

Processed foods make great use of a range of thickening agents, including gels, pectins, gums, starches, emulsifiers and seaweed derivatives such as agar, alginate and caragheenan. These ingredients help to bind fats to oils to prevent separation during long storage times, and bulk out the food by thickening cheap ingredients such as water. Cornflour is derived from maize, and so might be some starches and gums, and this maize could include GM maize. The emulsifiers may be derived from soya oil, which might be derived from GM soya. Gelatine is derived from cattle and pig skin, bones and connective tissue, and the concern here is whether the animals may have been fed with GM maize or soya feed (see Meat, above, and Gelatine, above).

☑ Green's Quick-Jel

❓ McDougall's Granules for Thickening (starch, vegetable oil, maltodextrin, lecithin)

☑ Supercook Vege-Gel

❓ Supercook Gelatine (?feed)

Tinned beans See Beans, tinned

Tinned fish (see also Fish and Fish fingers)

No GM fish are permitted to be sold in the UK, but the main concern with tinned fish is the medium in which the fish is prepared – which may include vegetable oils, tomato paste, or thickeners. The oil may be derived from maize or soya, including GM maize or soya, the tomato may come from GM tomato paste, and the thickening agents, such as modified starch, may be derived from maize starch, including GM-derived maize starch.

[?] Glenryck (tomato paste, vegetable or soya oil)
[?] John West (vegetable or soya oil)
[?] John West Tuna Light Lunch (modified cornflour, vegetable oil)
[?] Princes (tomato paste, vegetable or soya oil)

Tinned fruit

There are no GM fruits on sale in the UK. Tinned fruit may be packed in fruit juices or in syrup. Some syrup is made using glucose syrup, which can be derived from maize, including GM maize. Check the ingredients list on the label as the formulations may change from batch to batch. Fruit pie fillings may be thickened with starches derived from maize, including GM maize.

[✔] Del Monte fruits in juice, Fruitini
[?] Del Monte fruits in syrup (some include glucose syrup)
[✔] John West fruits in juice
[?] Morton's fruit pie fillings (modified starch)
[✔] Princes fruits in juice
[?] Princes fruits in syrup (some include glucose syrup)

Tinned meats (see also Meat products, Ready meals and Meat pies)

Animals from which tinned meat is derived may have been fed GM materials during their rearing (see Meat, above). Tinned meat may also contain added ingredients derived from GM material.

Processed meats may be prepared with added thickeners, emulsifiers and flavour enhances such as monosodium glutamate, and be sold in sauces containing similar ingredients and also tomato paste. All these may be derived from GM sources.

[?] Campbell's Meat Balls (?feed, rusk, modified starch, tomato paste)
[?] John West Pork Roll (?feed, starch, soya protein)
[?] Pek Turkey Breast (?feed)
[?] Princes Corned Beef/Pork Stuffing Roll/Ham (?feed)
[✘] Princes Pork Luncheon Meat (?feed, GM isolated soya protein)

[?] Princes Stewed Steak & Kidney (?feed, tomato paste, cornstarch, caramel colouring)
[?] Spam (?feed)
[?] Tyne Brand Irish Stew/Braised Beef/Mince & Onion (?feed, soya protein isolate, modified starch, caramel colouring)
[?] Ye Olde Oak Ham (?feed)
[?] Ye Olde Oak Turkey Roll (?feed, starch)

Canned/Tinned pasta See Pasta

Tinned puddings (see also Milk puddings)
Like cakes, these are made with starches, fats and sweetening agents that may include derivatives from maize and soya, including GM maize and soya.
[?] Heinz Jam Puddings (vegetable oil, modified cornflour)

☑ Tinned vegetables
Most tinned vegetables are prepared in a salt solution, possibly with the addition of chemicals that help retain the firm texture of the contents. (One chemical is lactic acid, which may be produced from genetic engineering in the near future, according to the US Agricultural Research Service.) Tinned mushy peas and other processed peas may have colouring added, as may some other vegetables.

Tofu
Tofu is a curd made from soyabeans, and the main concern is the source of the beans, as this might include GM soya crops.
☑ Cauldron tofu and marinated tofu
☑ Clear Spot
☑ Clearspring
☑ Dragonfly
☑ Granovita organic tofu
☑ Nature Made tofuburgers
☑ Redwood
☑ Taifun
☑ Yuksun

Tomatoes (See also Tinned vegetables)
Both tomato paste (from Zeneca) and fresh GM tomatoes
(Calgene's Flavr Savr) have been approved by UK government
advisers for food use in the UK, the first in 1995 and the second
in 1996. Zeneca's tomato paste was further approved for a
range of food products, such as pizza sauces, ketchup and
others, in 1996.

In the USA, the marketing of the Flavr Savr tomato – designed
to have an extended shelf-life – has been hindered by various
production and transport problems, and by the requirement of
retailers to label these fresh tomatoes as having been genetically
modified. It is believed that there are no Flavr Savr tomatoes on
general sale in the UK.

GM tomato purée appeared on British supermarket shelves
within months of government approval. Despite the fact that GM
tomato paste does not have to be labelled as such, these
products carried clear statements that the paste was from GM
tomatoes. They are now being phased out.

Apart from these two sources of GM tomato, there are no
others permitted for sale in the UK, but research is under way
into creating GM salad vegetables with greater resistance to
pests, greater tolerance of pesticide sprays, and slower
decaying properties giving them a longer shelf life and greater
transportation potential.

☑ all organic tomatoes and organic tomato purées, pastes and
tinned tomatoes
☑ fresh tomatoes, unless Flavr Savr
? other tomato pastes and purées

Tomato ketchup See Sauces

Tomato purée See Tomatoes

Tongue See Meat and Tinned meats

Tortillas, tortilla chips and nachos
A wheatflour-based flat bread, made with oil that might be

derived from maize or soya, including GM maize or soya.
Tortilla chips may be wheat or maize-based crisps, and nachos
are maize-based crisps – so both types of product may include
both maize and vegetable oil, which may be derived from GM
crops.

- ☑ Apache organic tortilla chips
- ❓ Discovery tortilla (vegetable oil, soya flour)
- ❓ Old El Paso nachos (maize, vegetable fat)
- ❓ Old El Paso tortilla (vegetable oil)
- ☑ TerraSana organic tortilla chips

Treacle
Treacle is based on cane sugar, which is not from GM canes.

- ☑ Tate & Lyle
- ☑ Essential molasses

Trifle See Desserts

Tripe See Meat

Trout See Fish

Truffles See Fungi or Chocolate and confectionery

Tuna See Fish and Tinned fish

Turkey See Chicken and turkey and Tinned meats

☑ Turnips
There are no GM turnips permitted for sale in the UK, but field
trials of GM turnips are being undertaken in the USA.

☑ Vanilla
There is no GM vanilla permitted for sale in the UK. Much of
today's vanilla flavour in processed foods is derived from vanillin,
a synthetic substitute for vanilla. The production of vanillin from
genetically modified bacteria is being researched.

Veal See Meat

Vegetable oil See Fats and oils

Vegetables (see also Frozen vegetables and Tinned vegetables)
There are no GM varieties of vegetables permitted to be sold in
the UK, with the exception of tomato paste from GM tomatoes
(see Tomatoes, above). Dried vegetables are usually prepared
without additional ingredients.
☑ Stamp vegetable chips
☑ TMI roasted vegetables
☑ Whitworth's Dried Vegetables Mix

Vegetarian products
Like other ready-prepared dishes (see Ready meals, above),
vegetarian dishes rely on various gums and starches to thicken
sauces and prevent them separating, and flavour boosters to
enhance the flavour of processed, long-shelf-life ingredients. The
vegetable oils, starches and gums, sweetening agents, colouring
agents, emulsifiers and flavour enhancers may be derived from
maize or starch, including GM maize and starch. Vegetarian
products also make use of meat substitutes, many of which are
derived from soya or maize flour – such as textured vegetable
protein and soya protein isolate, both of which can be derived
from GM sources. As from mid-1999, products carrying the
Vegtarian Society's V symbol have been approved by the Society
as being GM free, with the exception of GM chymosin used in
vegetarian cheeses.
❓ Aunt Bessie's Vegetarian Sausage Toad in the Hole (soya
protein isolate, vegetable oil, rusk, starch, hydrolysed vegetable
protein, lecithin)
☑ Bruno Fisher burger mixes
☑ Cauldron vegetarian burgers and sausages
❓ Dalepak Vegetarian burgers (vegetable oil, cheese,
breadcrumbs, hydrolysed vegetable protein, maltodextrin)
☑ Dragonfly bean burgers
☑ Essential textured vegetable protein

☑ Fabulous Foods Organic Vegetable Curry
❓ Goodlife Nut Cutlets (vegetable oil, soy sauce)
☑ GranoVita hot pot, burgers, sausages, frankfurters and soya protein
☑ Lee Kum Kee vegetarian sauces
❓ Linda McCartney dishes (vegetable oil, hydrolised vegetable protein)
❓ McIntosh Vegetarian Haggis (vegetable oil, caramel colouring)
❓ Morningstar Farms meat-free bacon strips (textured soya protein concentrate, soya oil, modified corn starch, riboflavin)
☑ Nature Made tofuburgers
☑ Pameer cheese-based meat substitute
☑ Proper Cornish vegetarian pastie
☑ Protoveg burger and sausage mixes
❓ Quorn Fillets, Sausages, Burgers, Lasagne, Chilli (?glucose syrup process, rusk, vegetable oil, starch, tomato purée)
❓ Quorn mince and pieces (?glucose syrup process)
☑ Realeat banger and burger mixes
☑ Redwood vegan
☑ Suma textured vegetable protein, burger and sausage mixes, nut roast
☑ Taifun organic
❓ Tivall vegetarian frankfurters, steaks (vegetable oil, starch, xanthan gum, riboflavin)
☑ Vegetarians Choice sausage/burger
☑ Vicsmix Vegetarian mix
☑ Western Fine Foods Countryburger

Vinegar

Vinegar is made from cider or wine, or from industrial acetic acid. Although a genetically modified brewing yeast was approved by UK government advisers in 1994, it is understood that this is not in widespread use for cider or wine.

☑ Aspall organic
☑ Byodo organic
☑ Clearspring organic
☑ Dufrais

☑ Martlet
☑ Sarsons

☑ Vine leaves

There are no GM vine leaves permitted for sale in the UK. Vine leaves are commonly sold ready stuffed with a concoction of rice, nuts and other ingredients – check the label to see the ingredients. Stuffed vine leaves may be bottled or canned in oil, in which case the oil may be from maize or soya, including GM maize or soya.

☑ Cypressa vine leaves in brine
☑ Zenia vine leaves

Vitamins and supplements

Vitamins and supplements should be sold with ingredients lists that show whether the product includes unspecified vegetable oils, starches, sweetening agents and flavourings that might be derived from soya or maize, including GM soya or maize. A survey by the Food Commission in 1998 found a range of garlic capsules from companies including Kwai, Superdrug, Hofels and Boots to be made with soya oil or unspecified vegetable oil. A calcium supplement from Boots was found to contain soya oil, and other calcium supplements (Calcia, Osteocare and Seven Seas Minerals for Bones) contained maize starch. There was no indication on the label about the source of these ingredients, which can be derived from GM crops.

Wafers See Cones and wafers

Waffles

Like pancakes, waffles contain flour, fat and sugar, and may include ingredients such as soya flour, glucose syrup and vegetable oils, which may be derived from soya or maize, including GM soya or maize.

❓ Ottoman waffles (lecithin, vegetable oil, soya flour, glucose syrup, fructose)
☑ Trafo organic

Walnuts See Nuts

Water See Mineral water

☑ **Water chestnuts** (see also Tinned vegetables)

☑ **Watercress**

☑ **Wheat**
There is no GM wheat permitted for sale in the UK, but research is under way on the use of genes from grasses and other plants to develop varieties of wheat that do not need to reproduce through pollination. Also being tested are GM wheat strains that have altered starch structure in the grains, designed at improving their suitability for noodles and pizza bases. Methods of increasing the gluten content of wheat to improve bread-making potential are being undertaken, using laboratory-created genes inserted into wheat cells. Bulgur wheat is made from cracked, partially cooked wheat.
☑ Crazy Jacks organic Bulgur wheat

☑ **Wheatgerm**
Wheatgerm is part of the wheat grain, and there is no GM wheat permitted to be sold in the UK.
☑ Bemax
☑ Froment
☑ Jordans

Whitebait See Fish

Whitener See Coffee creamers

Whiting See Fish

Wines See Alcoholic drinks

Winkles See Shellfish

Worcestershire Sauce (see also Sauces)
☑ Hammonds
☑ Lea & Perrins

☑ Yam

Yeast
UK government advisers approved the commercial use of a GM yeast for baking in 1990 and another yeast for brewing in 1994. It is understood that neither of these yeasts is in widespread commercial use at present, although in neither case would brewers or bakers be required to declare the presence of a GM yeast or GM yeast derivative on their labels.
☑ Allinsons Dried Yeast
☑ Be-Ro Dried Yeast
☑ DCL
☑ Hovis Dried Yeast

Yeast extract
Yeast extracts are usually derived from the by-products of the brewing industry. Because GM yeasts do not need to be labelled (see Yeast, above), it may be thought that GM yeasts could be present in yeast extracts, although brewing industry representatives say that GM yeasts are not in widespread use.
☑ Community Foods
☑ Essential yeast extract
☑ Mapletons Vitam-R
☒ Marmite (vegetable extract, riboflavin)
☑ Meridian

Yogurt and fromage frais (see also Desserts)
There are several concerns about the use of GM processes in the production of milk and milk products. For more on this, see the section on Milk, above. For food produced organically, dairy herds should not be fed GM-produced material. Some yogurts use thickeners such as starch, which can be derived from maize, including GM maize.

☑ all organically produced dairy foods
☑ GranoVita soya desserts
☑ Loseley yogurts
❓ Müller Crunch Corner (glucose, fructose, chocolate, maize)
❓ Müller Fruit Corner (dextrose, fructose)
❓ Munch Bunch Fromage Frais and Yogurts (starch)
☑ Onken Bio Pot Fruit Yogurt
☑ Plamil rice and soya desserts
☑ ProSoya soya-yogurt
☑ Provamil tofu-yogurt
☑ Rachels Dairy organic yogurt
❓ Shape Fromage Frais (fructose, modified starch)
❓ Skane Dairy Madal (vegetable oil)
❓ Ski Yogurt (oligofructose, modified starch)
☑ So Good soya desserts
☑ Woodlands Park sheep and goat yoghurt
☑ Yeo Valley organic
❓ Yoplait Petits Filous and Fromage Frais (glucose syrup, modified starch)

Yorkshire pudding

This is essentially a batter based on wheat flour, but may include vegetable oils, starches and thickeners based on soya or maize, including GM soya or maize. Frozen Yorkshire puddings may include unspecified vegetable oils, which might be derived from soya and maize, including GM soya and maize.
☑ Goldenfry Yorkshire Pudding Mix
☑ Original Yorkshire Pudding Mix
☑ Whitworth's Pancake and Yorkshire Pudding Mix

EATING OUT

This is a book about the food we can buy in the shops, but most people also eat out every now and then. So we asked the UK's major high-street restaurant chains about their policies, and for good measure we also examined school meals and meals-on-wheels services.

From September 1999, catering services must show on the menu or on a display whether any of their products contain GM soya or maize (but not the derivatives such as oils and starches). Alternatively, caterers can post up on a notice that their staff can answer questions about the presence of GM soya or maize. This is not a very satisfactory position for consumers or caterers, and many caterers are moving towards removing any ingredients that require GM declarations. Among the first were the caterers for MPs. The House of Commons Refreshment Department stated in July 1998 that it would 'avoid, wherever possible, the procurement of foods which contain genetically modified organisms'.

We cannot all eat at the House of Commons, so we asked some of the other large catering concerns in Britain what they were doing about GM foods. This is what they said. We have given a telephone number if you want to find their latest position.

Burger King
The company says it is 'actively working to remove GM ingredients and GM derivatives'. They could give us no exact timescale for this.
☎ 01895 206000 or customer helpline ☎ 0800 181 167

Caffé Uno
The company told us they were currently working to ensure their suppliers could confirm if there were any GM ingredients present in any product. The company wants to 'work towards totally GM free products'.
☎ 0171 930 9324

Domino Pizza
The company told us that 'Domino Pizza is to become a GM free zone'. They are currently having their products tested.
☎ 01908 580000

KFC
The company intends to remove GM ingredients at the earliest opportunity, but this may not include removing all derivatives from GM sources.
☎ 0171 580 2626

McDonald's
McDonald's said that the company is currently using up old stocks of products containing GM-maize ingredients (their fish fingers and fillets), and that in future McDonald's will not be using GM ingredients. This did not extend to GM derivatives 'as they cannot be detected'.
☎ 0181 700 7000 or their customer line ☎ 0990 244 622

Perfect Pizza
The company said 'We are about to declare our entire range GM free.' They did not clarify whether this includes GM derivatives.
☎ 01932 568000

Pizza Express
The company said their products are GM free, but they could not confirm their position on GM derivatives.
☎ 0181 960 8238

Pizza Hut
The company could not provide a statement on GM ingredients.
☎ 0171 580 2626

Prêt à Manger
The company has previously announced that it intends to remove GM ingredients from its products range, but could say little more at the time we went to press.
☎ 0171 827 6324

Starburger
The company could provide no comment, saying they had to contact their suppliers.
☎ 0181 801 6222

Wimpy

The company told us that it is their policy not to use any GM ingredients in any of their products, although there is 'a small possibility that some of our coatings and seasonings may contain ingredients derived from starch or oil from GM maize or soya ... We continue to work towards a situation in the future where we will be 100% GM free.'
☎ 01628 891 655

Meals on Wheels

Local authorities may be providing these meals from their in-house catering services, or they may be buying the meals in from suppliers. For the in-house services, the Local Government Association has called for a complete ban on GM foods provided by local councils (see School meals, below). Meals provided by outside caterers are most likely to be supplied by the Apetito Group, who told us, 'All our products are GM free. No GM-derived ingredients are used at all. To the best of our knowledge our products contain no GM ingredients.'
Apetito ☎ 01225 753 636

Pubs and canteens

These are serviced by a range of small and large catering suppliers. Among the largest is Brake Brothers, who told us their list is constantly changing.
Brake Brothers customer helpdesk ☎ 01233 206363

School meals

An increasing number of local authorities have declared that it will be their policy to remove GM ingredients from school meals. The Local Government Association, which represents many of the authorities in Britain, has called for a complete ban on GM foods provided by local councils. In response to this, the organisation representing the caterers, the Local Authority Caterers Association (LACA), has recommended to all its member caterers 'to instruct their suppliers to take all possible steps to source alternative GM free products, provided at no additional cost.'

For more details contact LACA on ☎ 01483 766777, fax 01483 751991.

Part 3
FURTHER
INFORMATION

Company contacts

In this section of the book we provide more information about companies, organisations and government departments, and make some suggestions for further reading.

You will find here:

● The food manufacturers we contacted and many of the other companies whose products are named in our guide, together with their customer information lines
● Contact details for biotechnology companies in the UK, trade associations and government departments
● Organisations that are concerned with aspects of genetically engineered food, including consumer, environmental, wildlife, health and development organisations
● Suggestions for further reading.

FOOD MANUFACTURERS

Company	Brands and products	Customer information
● Adams	meat products	01755 766161
● A G Barr	Irn-Bru, Tizer	0141 554 1899
● Alara	Wholefoods organic foods, muesli	0171 387 9303
● Allied Bakeries	Allinson, Sunblest, Mighty White, Kingsmill, HiBran, Vitbe	01784 451366
● Ambrosia (CPC)	canned desserts	01372 462181
● Amoy (Pullman)	sauces	01704 880686
● Anchor (now New Zealand Milk)	dairy products	0800 591 658 and 0171 240 8880
● Andutra Ltd	Betty Crocker, General Mills	01322 385588
● Archer Daniels Midland	soya trader, food ingredients	01322 443000
● Ashby	tea, coffee	01206 851500
● Askey	wafers	01296 27111

● Aspall	cider, vinegar	01728 860510
● Atora (McDougalls/RHM)	fats, packet mixes	01753 857123
● Aunt Bessie's	frozen foods	01482 223223
● Baby Organix/ Organix Brands	organic baby foods	0800 393511 and 01202 479701
● Barleycup	beverages	0171 474 0555
● Bart	spices	0117 977 3474
● Batchelors (Unilever)	instant soup, instant dishes	0345 581 215 and 0171 822 5252
● Baxters	soups	01343 820393
● Bernard Matthews	fresh and frozen meat products	01603 872611
● Be Ro (RHM)	baking ingredients	01753 857123
● Biona	organic foods	0181 395 9749
● Birds (Kraft Jacob Suchard)	dessert mixes frozen foods, ice cream,	01242 236101
● Birds Eye-Walls (Unilever)	sausages	01932 263000 and 0171 822 5252
● Bioforce	organic condiments, herbs, foods	01294 277344
● Bionova	organic salad dressings, mustard, foods	01373 812161
● Bisto (RHM)	packet sauces	01753 857123
● Boursin	cheese	0800 616026
● British Bakeries	Hovis, Mothers Pride, Nimble, Granary	01753 857123
● British Sugar	sugar, Silver Spoon	01733 63171
● Britvic	7-up, Tango	01245 261871
● Brooke Bond (Unilever)	teas, food products	0171 822 5252
● H P Bulmer	cider	01432 352000
● Burtons	biscuits, Wagon Wheels	01344 412121
● Buxted	frozen meat products	01845 577485
● Buxton Foods	snack foods, Stamp collection	0171 637 5505
● Cadbury	chocolate, hot drinks, cakes, Bournvita, Bournville	0121 458 2000
● Campbell's	soup, Freshbake, Fray Bentos, V-8 juice	01553 692266
● Cargill	grain shippers, soya shippers	01932 861000
● Carmel Foods	Kosher wines and foods	0171 790 5904

● Cauldron foods	tofu, vegetarian foods	01275 818448
● Chambourcy (Nestlé)	dairy foods	0181 686 3333 and 0800 000 030
● Chicago Town	frozen pizzas	01772 622458
● Chivers Hartley	Hartley jams, Moorhouse jams, Roses marmalade, Loyd Grossman sauces, Haywards pickles	01223 233333
● Clearspring	health foods	0181 749 1781
● Clipper	fairly-traded teas, coffee	01308 863344
● Coca-Cola Schweppes	Five Alive, Coca-Cola, Cherry Coke, Dr Pepper, Canada Dry, Kia Ora	(0800 389 0050) 0800 227711 and 01895 231313
● Colmans of Norwich	mustard, Robinsons drinks, Jif juice	01293 648000 and 01603 660166
● Community Foods	dried fruit, pulses, juices, Clipper tea	0181 450 9411
● ConAgra	agricultural supplies, corn products	0161 654 0001
● Courage (Scottish Courage)	beers and lagers	01784 466199
● Cow & Gate (Nutricia)	baby foods, baby drinks, diabetic foods	01225 768381
● Crazy Jack	organic foods, herbs	c/o 0181 450 9419
● Crosse & Blackwell (Nestlé)	canned food, sauces, frozen foods	0181 686 3333 and 0800 000 030
● Dairy Crest	dairy foods, spreads, Clover, Yoplait, Frijj	0181 910 4000
● Dalepak Foods	frozen foods	0800 854776 and 01677 424111
● Dalgety	Golden Wonder, Homepride, Spillers	0171 486 0200
● Percy Dalton	nuts	0181 985 9241
● Danish Bacon Co	fresh and cooked meats	01707 323421
● Danone	dairy foods, desserts	0181 675 1877
● Daylay	eggs for Hillsdown	01623 870384
● DCL Yeast	food processing ingredients	01259 769880
● De Rit	health foods, snacks	01422 885523
● Dietary Foods ltd	non-dairy whitener, sweeteners, low-salts	01353 720791
● Direct Foods (Haldane)	health foods	01908 211311

179

● Dolmio (Masterfoods)	sauces	01553 692222
● Doritos	snack foods	01734 306 666 and 0345 274777
● Doves Farm	cereal products	01488 684880
● Dr Stuarts	herbal drinks	01359 242208
● Dunn's River (Enco)	dried goods, sauces, spices, Nurishment	01707 272775
● Eden Organic Juices (Novartis)	fruit and vegetable juices	01923 266122
● Eden Vale	dairy products	01430 860377
● Ekoland	juices	0181 395 9749
● Encona (Enco)	sauces	01707 272775
● Equal Exchange	fair-traded health foods	0131 220 3484
● Essential (Essential Trading)	wholefoods supplier and own-label foods	0117 958 3550
● Eunature	organic pasta, sauces	0181 450 9411
● Evernat	wholefoods, confectionery	01932 354211
● Express Dairies	dairy products, food ingredients	01430 860377
● Fentimans	brewed drinks	01434 682300
● Ferrero	chocolates, spreads Nutella	01923 897282
● Findus (Nestlé)	frozen foods	0181 686 3333 and 0800 000 030
● Fray Bentos (Campbell's)	tinned meat products	01553 692266
● Freshbake (Campbell's)	frozen meat products	01553 692266
● Fyffes	fruit and vegetables	0171 487 4472
● Gales (Nestlé)	honey, spreads	01904 603806 and 0800 000 030
● Geest	fruit, vegetables, packed salads	01775 761111
● Gerber Foods	Sunpride juices, Gerber frozen foods	0181 446 1424
● Gluten Free Foods Ltd	gluten-free foods, wholefoods	0181 952 0052
● Goldenfry	packet mixes	01937 588631
● Granose (Haldane)	health foods	01908 211311
● GranoVita	health foods	01933 273717
● Green & Black	organic confectionery	0171 229 4452

● Greens (Homepride)	packet mixes	01858 414141
● Gusto	herbal drinks	0181 964 9093
● Häagen-Dazs	ice creams	01932 570011
● Haldane	Granose, Haldane, Realeat, So Good yogurts, Dietburger, Hera	01908 211311
● Hambledon Herbs	organic herbs	01823 401205
● Hartley (Chivers Hartley)	jams	01223 233333
● Haywards (Chivers Hartley)	pickles	01223 233333
● Heath and Heather	health foods	0151 522 4000
● Heinz	tinned soups, pasta, Weight Watchers frozen foods, canned baby foods, John West, Farley's, pet foods	(0800 692 6009) 0181 573 7757
● Here (Haldane)	vegetarian foods	01908 211311
● Herta (Nestlé)	cooked meats	0181 686 3333 and 0800 000 030
● Hipp	organic baby foods	01635 528250
● Homepride	sauces, mixes	01858 414141
● Horlicks (SmithKline Beecham)	beverages	0181 560 5151
● Horizon	Maryland biscuits	0151 678 8888
● HP foods (Danone)	sauces, ketchup, beans, vinegar, mustard, ready meals	01858 410144
● Infinity Foods	wholefoods suppliers, own-label health foods	01273 424060
● Island Foods (Cleone)	baked foods	0121 551 2772
● Jacobs Biscuits	crackers, Huntley & Palmer	01734 492000
● Jane Asher	cakes	0171 584 6177
● Joe Smokes	frozen foods	0181 533 3373
● John West	tined meat, fish, fruit etc	0151 236 8771
● Jordans	cereals, cereal bars, Crunchy, Frusli	01767 318222

● Jus-Rol	pastry	01289 307737
● Kallo	stock cubes, soya products, rice cakes	01428 685100
● Kellogg's	cereals, snacks	0800 626066 and 0161 869 2000
● Kerrygold	cheese, butter	01538 399111
● Kettle Foods	snack foods	01603 744788
● Kitchen Garden	health foods, herbs	01803 853579
● Knorr (CPC)	stocks and soups, snacks Taste Breaks	(0800 731 1411) 01372 462181
● KP foods (United Biscuits)	nuts, snack foods, Skips, Hula Hoops	0800 566 11203 and 0181 894 5600 and 0321 576887
● Kraft Jacobs Suchard	Dairylea, All Gold, Birds, Angel Delight, Kenco, Kraft, Maxwell House, Toblerone, Vitalight, Twiglets	01242 236101
● Lift (G Payne)	instant tea	0181 688 7744
● Linda McCartney (Ross Young's/ United Biscuits)	frozen vegetarian foods	0800 626697
● Linda McCartney's DairyLike (Haldane)	dairy substitute foods	01908 211311
● Loseley	dairy, ice cream	01483 571881
● Loyd Grossman (Chivers Hartley)	sauces	01223 233333
● Lucozade (SmithKline Beecham)	soft drinks	0181 560 5151
● Lyme Regis Foods	health foods, confectionery	01428 722900
● Lyons Cakes	baked goods	01226 286191
● Lyons Tetley	tea coffee	0181 578 2345
● Lyons Maid (Nestlé)	ice cream	01904 603806 and 0800 000 030
● McCain Foods	Frozen foods, pizza, chips	01723 584141
● McCormick (UK)	Schwartz spices, Hermesetas, Lo-Salt	01494 533456
● McDougalls (RHM)	flour, sauces	01753 857123

● Macsween	vegetarian haggis	0131 440 2555
● McVitie's (United Biscuits)	biscuits, Go Ahead, Penguin, TUC	0500 011710
● Manor Bakeries	Cadbury's cakes, Mr Kipling	01753 840401
● Marcantonio	wafers	0181 591 3399
● Mars Confectionery	confectionery and ice creams Mars, Twix, Bounty, Galaxy, M&Ms, Snickers, Maltesers	01753 550055
● Masterfoods	Dolmio, Uncle Bens, Tyne Brand	01553 692222
● Maxwell House (Kraft Jacobs Suchard)	coffee	01242 236101
● Mazola (CPC)	oils	01372 462181
● MD Foods	milk, butter, cheese, Lurpak	01132 440141
● Meridian	organic foods, sauces, oils	01490 413151
● Milupa (Nutricia)	babyfoods, baby drinks,	01225 711511
● Molle Skovly	organic, milk-free, gluten-free confectionery	01373 812161
● Moorhouse (Chivers Hartley)	jams	01223 233333
● Moy Park	chickens, meat products	01762 352233
● Mr Bean	soups, sauces	01798 812122
● Muller Dairy	yogurts and desserts	01630 692000
● Nairns	oat biscuits	0131 620 7000
● Nestlé UK	Buitoni pasta, Chambourcy, Herta, Findus, Lyons Maid, Nescafe, Rowntree, Crosse & Blackwell, Gales	0181 686 3333 and 0800 000 030
● New Covent Garden Soup	soups	0181 960 2229
● New York Bagel Co	bagels	01733 233405
● J N Nichols	Vimto, Hubba-Bubba	0161 998 8801 and 01942 272800
● Northern Foods	Eden Vale, Express Dairies, Fox's biscuits, Bowyers	0115 986 8231

● Novartis	agricultural inputs, beverages, Ovaltine, Options, Eden Juices	01923 266122
● Nutella (Ferrero)	chocolate-nut spread	01923 897282
● Nutricia	babyfoods, baby drinks, diet foods	01225 711511
● Ocean Spray	fruit, fruit drinks	0171 407 0756
● Old El Paso (Pillsbury)	Mexican foods	0800 591223
● Onken	Bio-yogurt, Frufoo	0181 876 4520
● Options, Ovaltine (Novartis)	hot beverages	01923 266122
● Orchid	Ame, Aqua Libra, Purdeys	0141 646 3000 or 01429 863534
● Oxfam	Traidcraft and own-label foods	01865 311311
● Pataks	sauces, Indian foods	01942 272300
● Pedigree Petfoods	Whiskas, Brekkies, Katkins, Kitekat, Sheba, Chappies, Chum, Bounce, Pal, Cesar	0800 738800 and 01664 411111
● Peperami (Van den Bergh)	salami	0800 446464 and 0171 822 5252
● Pepsico International (see also Britvic)	Pepsi, 7-Up, Tango, Idris	0181 332 0332
● Perkins Foods	chilled, frozen and fresh fruit	01733 555706
● Pillsbury	Old El Paso, Green Giant, Jus Rol	01895 206206
● Plamil	soy products, dairy-free foods	01303 850588
● Planters	nuts	01734 306 666
● Plumrose	canned and chilled meats	01482 659390
● Premier Biscuits	supplies Cadbury's Smash, Cadbury's chocolate spread and supermarkets	0151 678 8888
● Primula (Kavli)	processed cheeses, dips	0191 487 7146
● Princes	meat and fish products	0151 236 9282

● Procter & Gamble	Sunny Delight, Pringles	0800 146412 and 0191 279 2000
● Provamel	non-dairy drinks	0181 577 2727
● Purdeys (Orchid)	energy drinks	0141 646 3000 or 01429 863534
● Quaker Oats	cereals	0181 574 2388
● Quorn	vegetarian foods	0800 174 966 and 01642 710803
● Rachels Dairy	dairy foods	01970 625805
● Ralston Purina	petfood, Kit N Kaboodle, Cat Chow, Dog Chow, Bakers	01276 855135
● Realeat (Haldane)	meat substitutes, VegeMince	01908 211311
● Red Bull	energy drinks	0171 307 0000
● RHM Foods	Atora, Be-Ro, Bisto, Cerebos, McDougalls, Robertson's, Saxa, Sanatogen	(0800 366000) 01753 857123
● Ribena (SmithKline Beecham)	soft drinks	0181 560 5151
● Robertsons (RHM)	jams	01753 857123
● Robinsons Drinks (Colmans of Norwich)	fruit drinks	01603 660166
● Roche Products	vitamin supplements to the trade	01773 536500
● Roche Consumer Health	vitamin supplements to the public	01707 366000
● Roses (Chivers Hartley)	marmalades	01223 233333
● Ross Young's (United Biscuits)	frozen foods	01472 359111
● Rowntree (Nestlé)	Kit Kat, Smarties,	01904 604604 and 0800 000 030
● Ryvita	crispbreads	01292 743090
● St Ivel (Unigate)	spreads, Gold, Utterly Butterly, Vitalite, cheese, butter, Shape yogurts	01793 848444
● Schwartz (McCormick)	spices	01494 533456

● Schweppes Europe (see also Coca-Cola Schweppes)	soft drinks, Kia Ora, Sunkist	01923 210500
● Seven Seas	food supplements	01482 375234
● Sharwoods	sauces, spices	01784 473000
● Shippams (J M McCurrach)	meat products	0141 248 7596
● Shipton Mill	organic flour	01666 505050
● Silver Spoon	sugar, dessert toppings Treat	01733 63171
● SMA Nutrition	formula babymilks	01628 660633
● SmithKline Beecham	Ribena, Lucozade, Horlicks	0181 560 5151
● So Good (Sanatarium)	soya milk drinks	01892 512 818
● Spillers (Dalgety)	flour, petfoods Friskies, Chunky, Butch, Winalot, Felix, Arthurs, Go Cat, Choosy pet foods	0800 738 2273 or 01606 42822 and 0171 486 0200
● Stute	diabetic jams	0117 923 8823
● Suma	wholefoods supplier and own-label foods	01422 345513
● Sunita	wholefoods	0181 452 8465
● Sunrise	soya health foods	0161 872 0549
● Supercook	cooking ingredients, packet mixes	01977 684937
● Tate & Lyle	cane sugar, syrups and cornsyrups	0171 626 6525
● Tilda Rice	rice, Madhur Jaffrey products	01708 521133
● Tivall	vegetarian sausage, burgers	0181 801 6421 and 0181 420 1010
● Tofutti	frozen soya desserts	0181 861 4443
● Traidcraft	fair-traded foods, snacks	0191 491 0591
● Trebor Bassett	confectionery	01923 896565
● Twinings	tea, coffee	01264 334477
● Twin trading	coffee, chocolate	0171 375 1221
● Tyne Brand (Masterfoods)	meat products	01553 692222
● Uncle Bens (Masterfoods)	rice products, sauces	01553 692222

● Unigate	dairy foods, St Ivel	01793 848444
● Unilever	Van den Bergh, Walls, Birds Eye, Batchelors, Brooke Bond	0171 822 5252
● United Biscuits	McVitie's, Ross Young's, KP, Linda McCartney	0500 011710 and 01895 432100
● Van den Berghs (Unilever)	Flora, Delight, Crisp n Dry, Olivio, Blue Band, Stork	0800 446464 and 0171 822 5252 (0800 281029), (0800 454050)
● Village Bakery	baked goods	01768 881515
● Vimto (J N Nichols)	soft drinks	0161 998 8801
● Vinceremos	wines and spirits, organic drinks	0113 257 7545
● Walkers Snack Foods	crisps, Doritos, Planters nuts	01734 306 666 and 0345 274777
● Walls (Unilever)	ice cream, sausages	01932 263000 and 0171 822 5252
● Warburtons	bread, baked goods	0800 243684
● Weetabix	cereals, Weetos, Alpen, Ready Brek	01536 722181
● John West	canned fish, canned vegetables	0151 236 8771
● Westler	meat products, sauces	01653 693971
● Whitworth's	dried fruit and vegetables, grains	01933 653000
● Whole Earth Foods	organic canned foods, cereals, sauces, preserves	0171 229 7545
● Wrigleys	chewing gum	01752 701107
● Ye Olde Oak Foods	canned meats, soups	0171 231 3421
● Yeo Valley Farms	dairy	01761 462798
● Yoplait	dairy foods	0181 910 4000
● Young's (Ross Young's, United Biscuits)	frozen foods	0800 496 8647

BIOTECHNOLOGY COMPANIES

AgrEvo UK Ltd
Hauxton
Cambridge CB2 5HU
☎ 01223 870312
website: http://www.agrevo.com

Monsanto plc
PO Box 53
Lane End Road
High Wycombe
Bucks HP12 4HL
☎ 01494 474918
freephone ☎ 0800 092 0401
websites:
http://www.monsanto.co.uk
(for UK/European issues)
http://www.monsanto.com
(for global issues)

Novartis Consumer Health
Station Road
Kings Langley
Hertfordshire WD4 8LJ
☎ 01923 271517
website: http://www.novartis.com

Zeneca
15 Stanhope Gate
London W1Y 6LN
☎ 0171 304 5000
website: http://www.zeneca.com

TRADE ASSOCIATIONS

Food and Drink Federation
6 Catherine Street
London WC2B 5JJ
☎ 0171 836 2460
website:
http://www.foodfuture.org.uk

British Retail Consortium
5 Grafton Street
London W1X 3LB
☎ 0171 647 1500

Institute of Grocery Distribution
Grange Lane
Letchmore Heath
Watford
Herts WD2 8DQ
☎ 01923 857141
website: http://igd.org.uk

National Farmers Union
Agricultural House
164 Shaftesbury Avenue
London WC2H 8HL
☎ 0171 331 7200
website: http://www.nfu.org.uk

GOVERNMENT DEPARTMENTS

Ministry of Agriculture, Fisheries and Food (MAFF)
Whitehall Place
London SW1A 2HH
☎ 0171 238 6000
Helpline: t 0645 33 55 77
website: www.maff.gov.uk

Advisory Committee on Novel Foods and Processes (ACNFP)
ACNFP Secretariat c/o MAFF
☎ 0171 238 6244
website:http://www.maff.gov.uk/food/novel/acnfp.htm

Food Advisory Committee FAC Secretariat c/o MAFF
☎ 0171 238 6267
website:http://www.maff.gov.uk/food/fac/fachome.htm

Department of the Environment, Transport and the Regions (DETR)
Biotechnology Unit
Ashdown House
123 Victoria Street
London SW1E 8DE
☎ 0171 890 5277
website:http://www.environment.detr.gov.uk

Advisory Committee on Releases to the Environment (ACRE)
Secretariat: ☎ 0171 890 5277
website:http://www.environment.detr.gov.uk/acre/index.htm

USEFUL ORGANISATIONS

When contacting any of these organisations by post please include a large stamped addressed envelope.

Action Aid
Hamlyn House
Macdonald Road
Archway, London N19 5PG
☎ 0171 561 7561
website: http://www.actionaid.org

Action Against Allergy
PO Box 278
Twickenham TW1 4QQ
☎ 0181 892 2711

Baby Milk Action
23 St Andrew's Street
Cambridge CB2 3AX
☎ 01223 464 420
website:
http://www.gn.apc.org/babymilk

Campaign against GE School Dinners
1A Waterlow Road
London N19 5NJ
☎ 0171 272 4474
website:http://www.greenparty.org.uk

Catholic Institute for International Relations
Unit 3
Canonbury Yard
109a New North Road
London N1 7BJ
☎ 0171 354 0883
website: http://www.ciir.org

Christian Aid
PO Box 100
London SE1 7RT
☎ 0171 620 4444
website:http://www.christian-aid.
org.uk

Compassion in World Farming
5A Charles Street
Petersfield
Hampshire GU32 3EH
☎ 01730 264 208
website: http://www.ciwf.co.uk

Consumers' Association
2 Marylebone Road
London NW1 4DF
☎ 0171 830 6000
website: http:/www.which.net

Council for the Protection of Rural England
Warwick House
25 Buckingham Palace Road
London SW1W 0PP
☎ 0171 976 6433
website:http://www.greenchannel.
com/cpre

English Nature
Northminster House
Peterborough
PE1 1UA
☎ 01733 455000
website: http://www.english-nature.
org.uk

Food Labelling Agenda (FLAG)
PO Box 25303
London NW5 1WY

Food Commission
94 White Lion Street
London N1 9PF
☎ 0171 837 2250
website:http://ourworld.compuserve.
com/homepages/foodcomm.htm

Freeze Campaign
Genetic Engineering Alliance
94 White Lion Street
London N1 9OPF
☎ 0171 837 0642

Friends of the Earth
26-28 Underwood Street
London N1 7JQ
☎ 0171 490 1555
website: http://www.foe.co.uk

Genetic Engineering Network
PO Box 9656
London N4 4JY
☎ 0181 374 9516
website:
http://www.dmac.co.uk/gen.html

Gaia Foundation
18 Well Walk
London NW3 1LD
☎ 0171 435 5000

Genetics Forum
94 White Lion Street
London N1 9PF
☎ 0171 837 9229
website:
http://www.geneticsforum.org.uk

Genetix Food Alert
c/o Green City
23 Fleming Street
Glasgow G31 1PQ
☎ 0141 554 6099
website: http://www.essential-
trading.co.uk/genetix.htm

genetiX snowball
One World Centre
6 Mount Street
Manchester M2 5NS
☎ 01273 625 173
website:http://gn.apc.org/pmhp/gs

GeneWatch
The Courtyard
Whitecross Street
Tideswell
Buxton SK17 8NY
☎ 01298 871 898
website:http://www.genewatch.org

Greenpeace
Canonbury Villas
London N1 2PN
☎ 0171 865 8234
website:http://www.greenpeace.org

Henry Doubleday Research Association
Ryton on Dunsmore
Coventry CV8 3LG
☎ 01203 303 517
website: http://www.hdra.org.uk

Hyperactive Children's Support Group
71 Whyke Lane
Chichester
Sussex PO19 2LD
National Food Alliance (NFA)
see Sustain, the Alliance for Better Food and Farming

Pesticides Trust
Eurolink Business Centre
49 Effra Road
London SW2 1BZ
☎ 0171 274 8895
website:http://www.gn.apc.org/pesticidestrust

Royal Society for the Protection of Birds (RSPB)
The Lodge
Sandy
Bedfordshire SG19 2DL
☎ 01767 680551
website: http://www.rspb.org.uk

Royal Society for the Prevention of Cruelty
to Animals (RSPCA)
The Causeway
Horsham
W. Sussex RH1Z 1HG
☎ 01403 264181
website: http://www.rspca.org.uk

SAFE Alliance
see Sustain, The Alliance for Better Food and Farming

Soil Association
Bristol House
40-56 Victoria Street
Bristol BS1 6BY
☎ 0117 929 0661
website:
http://www.soilassocation.org

Sustain, the Alliance for Better Food and Farming
(formerly the National Food Alliance and SAFE)
94 White Lion Street
London N1 9PF
☎ 0171 837 1128

Student Environment Network
c/o Grassroots Office, UMU
Oxford Road
Manchester M13 9PR
☎ 0161 275 2942

Townswomen's Guilds
Chamber of Commerce House
75 Harborne Road
Edgbaston
Birmingham B15 3DA
☎ 0121 456 3435
website:
http://www.townswomen.org.uk

Vegetarian Society
Parkdale
Dunham Road
Altrincham
Cheshire WA14 4QG
☎ 0161 928 0793
website: http://www.vegsoc.org

World Development Movement
25 Beehive Place
London SW9 7QR
☎ 0171 737 6215
website: http://wdm.org.uk

The Wildlife Trusts
The Green
Witham Park
Waterside South
Lincoln LN5 7JR
☎ 01473 890 089
website:
http://www.wildlifetrust.org.uk

Women's Environmental Network
87 Worship Street
London EC2A 2BE
☎ 0171 247 3327
website:
http://www/gn.apc.org/wen

FURTHER READING

The Ministry of Agriculture, Fisheries and Food (MAFF) publishes a factsheet *Genetically Modified Food* (available from MAFF's helpline on ☎ 0345 335577) and a Foodsense leaflet *Genetic Modification and Food* (☎ 0645 556000)

The Food and Drink Federation produces a booklet, *Food for Our Future, Food and Biotechnology,* 1999 available from the Food and Drink Federation, 6 Catherine Street, London WC2B 5JJ (☎ 0171 836 2460)

The Consumers' Association's booklet, *Gene Cuisine: A Consumer Agenda for Genetically Modified Foods,* Consumers' Association Policy Report, 1997, is available by telephoning ☎ 01992 822800

Five Year Freeze on Genetic Engineering and Patenting in Food and Farming by Genetic Engineering Alliance (☎ 0171 837 0642)

Splice, the Magazine of the Genetics Forum: subscriptions from Genetics Forum, 94 White Lion Street, London N1 9PF (☎ 0171 837 9229)

The Ecologist magazine, The Monsanto Files, Vol 28, No 5, Sept/Oct 1998 (☎ 0171 351 3578)

The Food Magazine, published by the Food Commission, 94 White Lion Street, London N1 9PF (☎ 0171 837 2250)

BOOKS

Eat Your Genes: How Genetically Modified Food is Entering our Diet, Stephen Nottingham, Zed Books Ltd,1998

Biopiracy by Vandana Shiva, Green Books, 1998 (Green Books ☎ 01803 863260)

Genetic Engineering: Dream or Nightmare? The Brave New World of Bad Science and Big Business. Dr Mae-Wan Ho, Gateway Books, 1998

Against the Grain: The Genetic Transformation of Global Agriculture, Mark Lappé and Britt Bailey, Earthscan, 1999

The Biotech Century: Harnessing the Gene and Remaking the World, Jeremy Rifkin, Tarcher and Putnam (New York), 1998

Engineering Genesis: the Ethics of Genetic Engineering in Non-Human Species, edited by Donald Bruce and Ann Bruce, Earthscan Publications Ltd, 1998

Theology and Biotechnology: Implications for a New Science, Celia Deane-Drummond, Geoffrey Chapman (Cassell), 1997

Improving Nature? The Science and Ethics of Genetic Engineering, Michael J Reiss and Roger Straughan, Cambridge University Press, 1996

Organic

Where to Buy Organic Food, from the Soil Association, Bristol House, 40-56 Victoria Street, Bristol, BS1 6BY
(☎ 0117 929 0661)

The Organic Directory, edited by Clive Litchfield, Green Books
(☎ 01803 863260)

The Shoppers Guide to Organic Food, Lynda Brown, Fourth Estate, 1998

General

What the Label Doesn't Tell You, Sue Dibb (Thorsons), 1998

The Food We Eat, Joanna Blythman (Penguin), 1998

FOOTNOTES

1 Greenberg Consultants, 'Strategy Report to Monsanto UK', 5 October 1998.
2 *Financial Times*, 18 February 1999.
3 Monsanto website: www.monsanto.co.uk.
4 Julian F Burke and Sandy M Thomas, 'Agriculture Is Biotechnology's Future in Europe', *Nature Biotechnology*, Vol. 15, August 1997.
5 *Financial Times*, 5 February 1999.
6 'Report of the Working Party on the Experimental Manipulation of the Genetic Composition of Micro-organisms', Cmnd 5880, January 1975.
7 'Government Rejects Fresh Demands for Moratorium', *Financial Times*, 13 February 1999.
8 'GM Food Advisers Shake-up Planned', *Independent*, 15 February 1999.
9 *Financial Times*, 13 February 1999.
10 ACRE Newsletter, No. 7, June 1997.
11 'Breakdown of UN Talks on Genetically Modified Crops Threatens Trade Tensions', *Financial Times*, 26 February 1999.
12 *Dispatches*, Channel 4, 11 March 1999.
13 Quoted in S Nottingham, *Eat Your Genes*, Zed Books, 1998.
14 House of Lords Select Committee on European Communities, 'EC Regulation of Genetic Modification in Agriculture', December 1998.
15 Quoted in 'How Safe Is GM Food?', *Woman's Own*, 8 March 1999.
16 'Public Might Have Been Misled on Beef Threat', *The Times*, 7 November 1999.
17 NOP Poll for the *Independent on Sunday*, 21 February 1999.
18 The Soil Association, 'Genetic Engineering: The Impact on Environment and Wildlife', Briefing Paper, 1998.
19 Advisory Committee on Releases to the Environment, 'The Commercial Use of Genetically Modified Crops in the United Kingdom: The Potential Wider Impact on Farmland Wildlife', Department of the Environment, Transport and the Regions, 1999.
20 'The Risk of Crop Transgene Spread', *Nature*, 7 March 1999.
21 Advisory Committee on Releases to the Environment, op. cit.
22 Department of the Environment, Transport and the Regions, Press Release 5599, 3 July 1998.
23 Dr Jean Emberlin et al., 'A Report on the Dispersal of Maize Pollen', National Pollen Research Unit, University College, Worcester, February 1999.
24 Soil Association, 'Government Advice on Genetic Contamination Challenged by New Independent Report', Press Release, 2 March 1999.
25 Speaking at the Lady Eve Balfour Memorial Lecture, 1996.
26 Committee on the Ethics of Genetic Modification and Food Use, Report, MAFF, 1993.
27 Consumers' Association, 'Gene Cuisine: A Consumer Agenda for Genetically Modified Foods', 1997.
28 RAFI website: www.rafi.org.uk.
29 Consumers' Association, op. cit.
30 Monsanto Posilac Product Information Leaflet, see *The Food Magazine*, Issue 25, Vol. 3, The Food Commission, 1994.
31 *Nature*, 388:311, 24 July 1997.
32 S Nottingham, *Eat Your Genes*, Zed Books, 1998.
33 Ibid.
34 '"Modify GM Food Labelling" Says *Which?*', Press Release, Consumers' Association, 2 March 1999.
35 'Genetic Corn in Healthfood', *Daily Telegraph*, 5 February 1999.
36 *Daily Mail*, 16 February 1999.
37 'Scientists Find Banned Soya in UK Products', *Independent on Sunday*, 14 February 1999.